Old GREENOCK

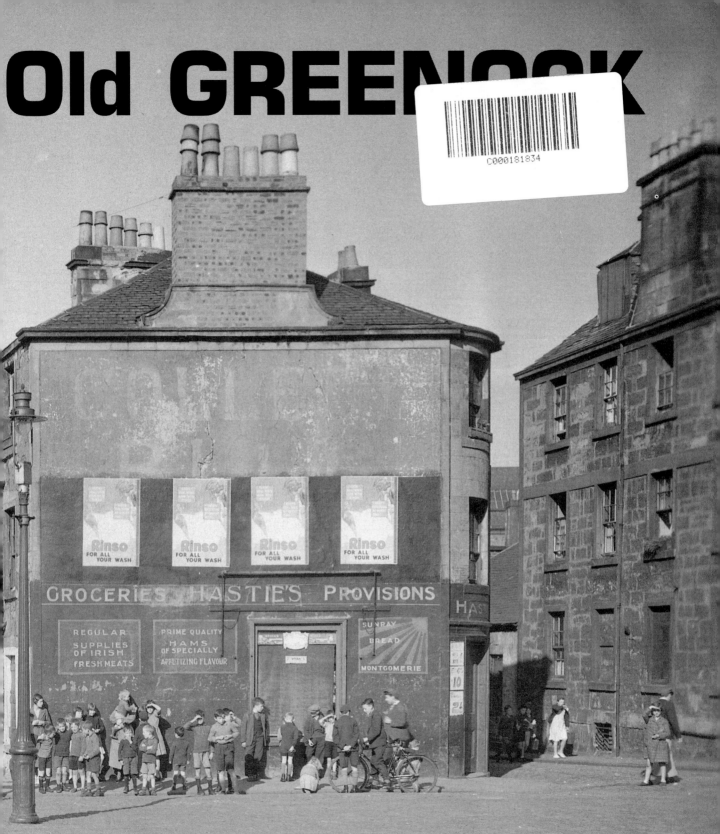

Joy Monteith

Stenlake Publishing Ltd.

2004

© Joy Monteith 2004
First published in the United Kingdom, 2004,
reprinted 2005, 2007
by Stenlake Publishing Ltd.
Telephone: 01290 551122
Printed by St Edmundsbury Press, Bury St Edmunds, IP33 3TZ

ISBN 9781840333145

ACKNOWLEDGEMENTS

The author would like to thank the many people who helped with information about individual photographs. Particular thanks are due to Sandra Macdougall of Inverclyde Libraries and Betty Hendry of the Watt Library for providing generous assistance with research material, and to Oliver van Helden of Stenlake Publishing for editorial support and technical advice.

The publishers would like to thank the following people for permission to reproduce pictures. Norman Burniston: pages 7 (lower), 56 (upper), 78 (upper) and 80 (upper); Mrs E. Hall: pages 8 (lower) and 42–43; Robert Kelly: page 14 (upper); Mrs P. Kerr: page 71; John Pow: page 57 (lower); George Simpson: pages 17 (lower), 47–53 and 54 (upper). Many of the images in this book come from the collection held by Inverclyde Libraries, and remain within their copyright (or that of the original photographer). Stenlake Publishing gratefully acknowledges the assistance of Inverclyde Libraries and other copyright holders in making photographs available for this book.

FURTHER READING

The books listed below were used by the author during her research. None of them is available from Stenlake Publishing. Those interested in finding out more are advised to contact their local bookshop or reference library.

Dow, James L., *Greenock*, 1975
Hamilton, T. W., *How Greenock Grew*, 1947
Macdougall, Sandra, *Profiles From the Past*
Monteith, Joy, & Anderson, Matt, *Greenock From Old Photographs*, 1980
Monteith, Joy, & McCarroll, Janette, *Greenock From Old Photographs, Vol. 2*, 1983
Smith, R. M., *The History of Greenock*, 1921
Williamson, George, *Old Cartsburn*, 1894
Williamson, George, *Old Greenock*, 1886
Williamson, George, *Old Greenock*, second series, 1888
Greenock Advertiser
Greenock Telegraph
Greenock post office directories
Statistical Accounts of Scotland: Parish of Greenock 1793, 1836–42, 1962

This early photograph, dating from *c*.1860, looks eastwards along Nelson Street and shows the original Greenock Academy building on the left. In 1847 it had been agreed that a new academy should be built by public subscription to incorporate the existing grammar school and the mathematical school. By 1852 a two-acre site had been acquired at Nelson Street and Messrs Hay, architects, of Liverpool, were engaged to design the new school. Greenock Academy opened on 3 September 1855 and promised to provide a course and style of instruction hitherto not enjoyed in Greenock. At the time the academy was surrounded by fields, and the West Burn flowed openly on the opposite side of the street. At the corner of Inverkip Street (foreground) was an orchard which the academy pupils enjoyed raiding from time to time. The school moved to its new location at Madeira Street in 1964, and the former site is now occupied by the James Watt College. The building with the distinctive spire on the other side of Nelson Street is the new West Church, now St Luke's, described on page 63.

INTRODUCTION

Unlike many other Scottish towns, Greenock – historically speaking – is a settlement of comparatively modern origins, which experienced exceptional growth over a relatively short period of 250 years or so.

Its beginnings lie in the small fishing village which clustered around the mouth of the West Burn on land which was owned by the Schaw family. In 1589 John Schaw was granted a charter by King James VI to build a parish kirk for the 'poor people upon his lands who were all fishers, and of a reasonable number'. The construction of the church later known as the Old West Kirk provided a focal point for the village, which began to grow as a more settled community.

In 1635 Greenock was created a burgh of barony, a change in status which included the right to hold a weekly market on Fridays, as well as two fairs annually. Around the same time the natural advantages of the bay at Greenock began to encourage visits from the increasing volume of seaborne traffic on the River Clyde, and the place began to grow in size and importance.

By 1701 the population had reached 746, and was prospering from the strength of the herring trade. A decade later two innovations emerged as a result of this trade which were to have a major impact on the future development of the town. In 1710 the townspeople completed the construction of a harbour facility which would allow improved access to Greenock for shipping, and in 1711 John Scott started building fishing boats known as herring busses at the mouth of the West Burn, laying the foundation for the growth of shipbuilding and associated industries in the area.

Over the next century foreign and coastal trade increased rapidly, resulting in the establishment of a custom house at Greenock. Imports came from the West Indies, America, the Mediterranean and the Baltic, while herring was still an important source of wealth to the town and was exported widely, along with coal and Scottish manufactured goods. At the same time, in addition to shipbuilding, other industries emerged, notably sugar refining, coopering, rope making and sailcloth manufacturing.

The opportunities for employment created by these enterprises encouraged an influx of people from the Highlands, particularly Argyll, to work as labourers, fishermen and sailors. By 1801 Greenock's population was 17,450 and it was estimated that three quarters of the town's population were native-born Highlanders, many of whom contributed to educational and literary progress in the town.

The nineteenth century saw unprecedented development in the provision of harbour facilities, making Greenock the principal port in Scotland by 1840. It also had the largest sugar refining industry in the country, the second largest shipbuilding industry, plus iron foundries, potteries, tanneries, woollen manufactories and cotton works, paper mills, grain mills, and unusually a straw hat manufactory.

By 1841 the population had doubled again to 35,921, and continued to rise steeply over the next seventy years, particularly as large numbers of immigrants from Ireland arrived, attracted by the prospect of obtaining work in the town. At the end of the nineteenth century the number of inhabitants stood at 68,217, supporting a large infrastructure of services including banks, shops, offices, theatres, newspapers and tramways, as well as schools and churches.

In tandem with this population growth, a number of large-scale public works were undertaken by various agencies throughout the nineteenth century. These projects included the recurrent and extensive construction of harbours and docks, the building of a new and elegant custom house, the introduction of the Shaws water supply, the arrival of a railway service and the provision of grandiose municipal buildings, reflecting an era of great civic pride.

However, the speed and nature of Greenock's phenomenal growth brought in its wake major problems of overcrowding, substandard housing, poverty and poor health, and during the mid-nineteenth century it had the unenviable reputation of being the unhealthiest town in Scotland. The majority of the population lived within the limits of the town centre which had grown around the original West Harbour. Almost every square inch of the twenty acres of land around the harbour had been built upon, and over the years properties had been subdivided and backland developments added, resulting in very low standards of living for a great many people.

Whilst the first limited efforts at slum clearance were made by the local authority in 1877, it was not until after 1919 that major council housing schemes began to appear away from the central area. Indeed one result of Greenock's haphazard pattern of growth meant that provision of sufficient and adequate housing remained a problem for the council well into the twentieth century.

Greenock's growth was accelerated by many exciting innovations in trade, industry and commerce, which over the years led to great changes to its original layout. However, the consequences of the town's history brought the most dramatic changes in the twentieth century. The original West Harbour of 1710 was filled in during the 1920s, changing the face of the town centre. In addition, various housing programmes cleared the old central area of its congested and unhealthy dwellings, and replacement housing on the outskirts of the town altered its shape and boundaries. Change also extended to the former shopping area based on Hamilton Street, which was replaced by a covered mall in the 1970s.

Some of the most far-reaching and dramatic changes stemmed from the decline of Greenock's historic industrial bases of shipbuilding, engineering and sugar refining, and their ultimate disappearance from the town by the 1990s with the loss of thousands of jobs. The majority of sites formerly occupied by these industries have been cleared, and in many cases redeveloped so extensively that their former locations are now unrecognisable.

New industries and major environmental improvements have emerged to offset the legacy of Greenock's remarkable past. Greenockians retain a strong pride in their industrial and maritime heritage and the Clydeside town which it shaped, and this selection of photographs will hopefully provide an insight into this fascinating heritage, as well as presenting a record of many of the changes which have taken place throughout Greenock's unique and absorbing history.

Greenock's origins stem from a small fishing community with a few houses scattered along the shore of the River Clyde from the mouth of the West Burn to the area called the Row-end. As the community developed towards the end of the sixteenth century, an informal boundary of Greenock town proper was formed by the West Burn to the west and the Delling Burn to the east. Running east from the Delling Burn to approximately the line of modern-day Sinclair Street was the separate community of Cartsdyke, which for a time was regarded as of greater importance than Greenock. Beyond that there were few developments in the area upriver to Inch Green, where the boundary between Greenock and Port Glasgow was eventually fixed. (Inch Green was originally a small island which was joined to the shore at low tide.) This photograph looks towards Greenock's eastern boundary from Bogston Farm, and was taken c.1933 just before work started on the new housing estate at Gibshill.

This 1883 view looks west from Inch Green towards Ladyburn and the two kilns of the Clyde Pottery. Here the river is full of timber, which was tied together with ropes and floated along the Clyde, where it would be stored on the water in timber ponds until required. The Clyde Pottery was established in 1814 and two of its original partners were James and Andrew Muir, who had started a straw hat factory at the Glebe in central Greenock in 1808. Between about 1820 and 1860 a second pottery, the Ladyburn Pottery, operated nearby at Garvel Park, with occasional ownership links to the Clyde Pottery, which was finally wound up at the end of 1905. On the left is Ladyburn Church, dating from 1875. The Ladyburn tan works were formed in 1805 on the banks of the burn, and were still operating during the First World War when they pioneered the use of sheepskins for use in aviators' jackets, car-coat linings and trench gloves.

A significant factor in the history of Greenock was the development of a series of harbours, notably the West Harbour in 1710, the East India Harbour in 1805, the Victoria Harbour in 1850, and the major project at Garvel Park in the 1870s and 80s which was to become the James Watt Dock, the Great Tidal Harbour and the Garvel Basin. Garvel House was built c.1777 by Bailie James Gammell, a local businessman who was one of the partners in the town's first bank, the Greenock Bank. At that time he lived in a large

town house in Cathcart Square, but built a second home in extensive parklands at Garvel as a country residence. The feu for Garvel Park was later acquired by John Scott, and in 1867 he sold the parklands to the Greenock Harbour Trustees for £80,000. The first phase of the development was the construction of the graving (dry) dock in 1874 at a cost of £89,000. Some twelve years later in 1886 the entire project was completed, leaving Garvel House (centre) surrounded by an extensive complex of docks and quays.

The proposal to build new harbours and docks at Garvel Park was not without controversy, but the project finally got underway with the appointment in 1869 of the engineer W. R. Kinniple of London to lay out the ground. It was almost ten years later, in June 1878, that the harbour trustees decided to proceed with the James Watt Dock element of the project. The foundation stone was laid on 6 August 1881 before an estimated crowd of 30,000 people who had processed

through the town beforehand, and the event coincided with the laying of the foundation stone for the municipal buildings. The James Watt Dock opened five years later on 5 August 1886, an event which was considered at the time to be the greatest occasion in the history of Greenock and its harbours. With a length of 2,000 feet, width of 300–350 feet, and a depth at high water of 32 feet, it allowed vessels of great tonnage to be kept constantly afloat.

Eleven acres of ground in the south-east of Greenock were donated to the town by Sir Hugh Shaw Stewart for the creation of the Lady Octavia Park, named after Sir Hugh's mother who had died in 1921. The daughter of the Marquis of Westminster, Lady Octavia Grosvenor married Sir Michael Shaw Stewart – with whom she had five sons and two daughters – in 1852. Taken from the park, this view looks towards the council housing built by Greenock Corporation under the various housing Acts introduced from 1919 onwards. Under the 1919 (assisted) scheme 114 houses were built at Bridgend; 128 were built under the 1924 scheme at South Craigieknowes; and via the 1930 and 1935 slum clearance Acts seventy houses were built at Grosvenor and 126 at Auchendarroch.

Built to provide material for the Clyde Pottery (p4), this flint mill was situated on the banks of the Carts Burn on Kilmacolm Road, near Auchmountain Glen. Flints were heated at high temperatures to calcine them, then mixed with water and ground between two millstones powered by the Carts Burn. The resultant mixture was then dried over brick stoves and transported in barrels to the pottery. At about 11 p.m. on 21 November 1835 the mill narrowly escaped being destroyed by the huge volume of water which thundered down the Carts Burn after Beath's Dam burst. The force of the water demolished the casing of the mill wheel and covered the wheel in debris and mud, but the mill and mill house survived. Further down the burn, in Cartsdyke, the torrent resulted in the loss of 38 lives. In Stanners Street several families were drowned in their beds. Subsequently damages of £4,200 were awarded against the Shaws Water Company for the failure of the dam.

The idea of bringing the beauty spot at Auchmountain Glen to wider notice was conceived during a severe trade slump in 1887. At that time the glen was in a wild state and choked with vegetation. Half a dozen local unemployed men started to put the ground in order, and when Sir Michael Shaw Stewart heard of the project he personally encouraged them to continue with their work. As a result, a pathway was constructed from Kilmacolm Road to the top of the Whinhill by the 'Auchmountain Boys', together with facilities such as a wooden clubhouse (illustrated here), aviary and greenhouse located near the glen's entrance. Various gardens and wells were also laid out along its length. Auchmountain Glen was regularly maintained over many summers and celebrated its jubilee in 1937. In later years it became neglected, but more recently has been the subject of community clean-up campaigns to reinstate the path.

Belville Street and Lauriston Street began to be developed in the late 1870s to provide housing close to the shipyards and associated industries which were expanding in the east end of the town. Prior to this, one of the few houses in the area was Belville House, home of Robert Allen of the Clyde Forge. The name Lauriston Street reflects the local connection with the Crawfurd family of Cartsburn. Lauriston Castle was the property of Mr McKnight Crawfurd, and portraits and antiques from the Cartsburn estate were removed to Lauriston when Cartsburn mansion house was demolished. In March 1970 a report condemned 95 houses in Lauriston Street as substandard, and as a result Greenock Corporation compulsorily purchased properties at 3–17 and 19 Lauriston Street and 86 Belville Street, plus a yard and shops at Barnhill Street. The area was eventually cleared and much of the site is now occupied by open space. This picture looks along Lauriston Street with Belville Street in the foreground.

This photograph is labelled 'Belville Place top class 1965' and was probably taken when the school was scheduled for closure and demolition. When the Education (Scotland) Act 1872 came into operation the town possessed 37 schools, but despite this, of 9,900 children over five and under thirteen years, 2,871 were not attending school. The newly formed school board erected two schools – in Mearns Street and Belville Street – without delay, the first of a series of well-equipped and commodious facilities located in the most densely populated areas of the town. Belville Place School opened on 8 August 1876 and cost £10,320 16s., with accommodation for 752 pupils and fees on a scale from eight pence to two shillings. At its opening it was stated that pupils would be urged to cultivate habits of cleanliness and good manners and would be taught 'useful rather than ornamental sewed work'.

The tenements at 37 and 43/45 Belville Street suffered severe damage during the Greenock Blitz of May 1941. Belville Street was hit on the first night's raid on 6 May, and a considerable number of people were killed in these three tenements, as well as further along at Lauriston Street and St Lawrence Street. In January 1961 the town council agreed in principle to a massive redevelopment plan for the Belville Street/St Lawrence Street area. Proposals included a number of maisonettes and (originally) nine blocks of multi-storey flats intended to replace 465 existing homes in the area with 714 modern ones. The cost was estimated to be £2 million. The first phase of new flats at St Lawrence Street was completed by 1964, and the redevelopment continued over the next ten years or so.

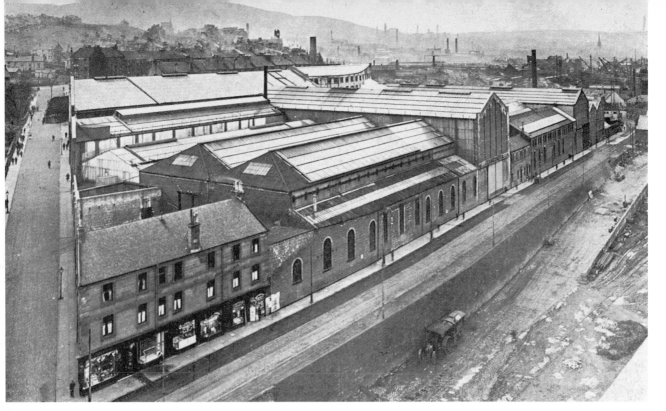

The firm of John G. Kincaid & Co., marine engineers and boilermakers, was formed in 1868 when John Kincaid, in partnership with John Hastie and Robert Shaw Donald, purchased the Clyde Foundry & Engine Works at East Hamilton Street. By 1888 the latter partners had left and the firm was known as Kincaid & Co. John Kincaid had served an apprenticeship at Caird & Co.'s engine works in Arthur Street, which he acquired in 1919, allowing considerable expansion potential. Throughout its history the firm was known both for its quality in production and its innovations in marine engineering. At the outset production was geared to steam engines, but Kincaid's was quick to appreciate the significance of diesel engines, and obtained its first order for a Burmeister & Wain engine in 1924 from Harland & Wolff. In 1953 new premises were built in Arthur Street, and the firm, which celebrated its centenary in 1968, constantly updated plant and production methods. However, as shipbuilding and marine engineering declined, Kincaid's was nationalised in 1972. After the break-up of British Shipbuilders the firm became Clark Kincaid, Kvaerner Kincaid, and most recently SKV Kincaid Ltd. Eventually all engine-building ceased, and over a period of time Kincaid's extensive premises have been demolished.

Main Street developed as the principal thoroughfare through Cartsdyke, a community which lay roughly within the area bounded by the Carts Burn on the west, Ratho Street on the east, and from the river back to the line later taken by Belville Street. By the end of the nineteenth century, hundreds of families lived in Main Street alongside a variety of commercial and industrial premises. This 1923 photograph looks west towards Knowe Road. To the left of the tram, and about to be demolished, are the so-called 'Lighthouse Tenements', originally eight in number and known to have been built by 1705. The name derived from speculation that at night light from these tenement windows acted as a beacon for fishermen returning to Cartsdyke Harbour. Also in this vicinity at 36 Main Street was the home of Jean Adam, who was born in 1704 and is regarded as the author of the poem The Mariner's Wife, best known for its refrain 'There's nae luck aboot the hoose'.

In 1933, under the powers of the 1930 Housing (Scotland) Act, designed to speed up the removal of slum houses, Greenock Corporation obtained a compulsory purchase order for the clearance of housing in the John Street area. The site designated to be cleared included the triangle of streets to the south of Main Street bounded by Arthur Street, St Lawrence Street and Cartsburn Street. This had been part of both the Cartsburn estate and the historic and distinct village of Cartsdyke, which remained a separate burgh from Greenock until 1840 (indeed at one time its harbour facilities were regarded as of greater importance than those of Greenock). This general view showing the area lying to the north of John Street and St Lawrence Street was taken from Serpentine Walk.

The junction of John Street and Crescent Street.

A back view of tenements at 23–27 John Street and 9 St Lawrence Street showing some of the dilapidation in the properties. The first feus in Cartsdyke were granted in 1671 in favour of Andrew Simpson and Elizabeth Crawfurd for ground on the shore, and the following year Mr Crawfurd of Cartsburn built a new mansion house on the banks of the Carts Burn near where Ingleston Street was later formed. Following this, one of the earliest parts of Cartsdyke to be further developed was the lane which became known as Stanners Street. This name was thought to be derived from the word 'standards', resulting from the fact that a shed for the official inspection of weights and measures using standard weights was situated in the street.

Arthur Street looking north from St Lawrence Street. Throughout the eighteenth and nineteenth centuries, further building of property and laying out of streets took place, leading in time to considerable congestion and overcrowding in the relatively small geographic area. By the time of the compulsory purchase order (1933), many people lived in unacceptable housing conditions, with low-rental accommodation consisting mainly of one- or two-apartment houses which were both badly maintained and had few amenities. Following clearance of the area some new houses were built after 1943, while other parts of the ground were used for industrial premises.

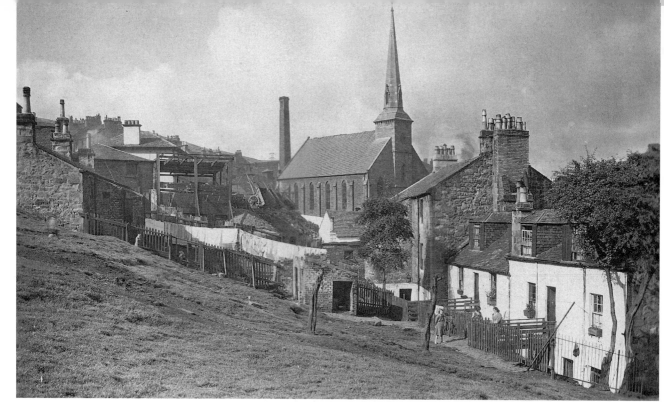

The former Cartsburn Augustine Church, built on land donated by the Crawfurd family and opened on 16 November 1856, is prominent in this back view of 4–10 St Lawrence Street. The church's congregation had been established some years previously from association with the East Kirk, and met in a building at Charing Cross until sufficient funds had been raised for a new building. Latterly known as Cartsdyke Church, the building was closed in 2003 due to extensive structural deterioration, and a new charge of East End of Greenock was formed, awaiting new premises.

John Street looking north-west.

David McEwing's painter's business in Arthur Street first appears in local trades directories in 1879/80. Over the years the entries record various addresses for the business in the street, including No. 14 in 1883, No. 10 in 1900 and No. 4 in 1915, when Mr McEwing is described as a painter and decorator. By 1931 the business was located at 7 Arthur Street and included the term 'dry-salter' (a dealer in dyes, gums, drugs, oils and sometimes pickles and tinned meats). In the last entry noted at the same address in 1963/64, the business is described as D. McEwing Hardware.

The firm of Scott & Co. (later Scotts' Shipbuilding & Engineering Co. Ltd.) had a long and eminent association with Greenock, and in its time had the distinction of being the oldest family firm to have been continuously in business. It was founded in 1711 by John Scott, who started building herring busses and other small vessels at a yard situated at the mouth of the West Burn. By 1787–9 the firm was constructing larger vessels, and as a result purchased more ground, extending its yard to the West Quay. In the early nineteenth century Scotts' were quick to adopt the introduction of steam propulsion, and by 1816 had built two of the earliest Clyde steamers, *Active* and *Despatch*. They also took the credit for the first Clyde-built steam frigate for the British navy, HMS *Greenock*, launched in 1849. By 1850 Scotts' had acquired a yard at Cartsdyke, and under the partnership of John Scott IV and his brother Robert Sinclair Scott the firm made significant progress in the development of the steamship and the multiple expansion engine. They bought Steele's shipbuilding yard and dry dock, where they established the Cartsburn yard and fitted it out for naval construction, selling the original yard to the west (which eventually became Caird's shipyard). Scotts' contribution to the history of naval architecture and marine construction is unparalleled, and the company constructed a huge range of vessels from clippers to merchant steamships, warships and offshore vessels. In 1969 it amalgamated with Lithgow's of Port Glasgow to become Scott Lithgow Ltd., which in turn became part of the nationalised British Shipbuilders Corporation in 1977. The last vessel to be built at the Cartsburn yard, the seabed operations ship *Challenger*, was launched in 1981, and by 1983 large-scale redundancies had been announced. The following year, as part of the government's privatisation programme, Scott Lithgow was sold to Trafalgar House and finally ceased to trade in 1993. The Cartsburn yard was demolished and the area redeveloped as a business site, leaving the graving dock as the only reminder of the formerly extensive industry which dominated this location, and which together with marine engineering had at one time employed 27.5 per cent of Greenock's working population. The main picture shows the view over Scotts' canteen at the Knowe, illustrating much of the extensive site; the smaller picture shows Scotts' Cartsburn dockyard offices.

Charing Cross, Greenock.

67920. J.V.

Scotts' gate at the Cartsburn yard stood in the area known as Charing Cross, seen here from Rue End Street looking east to Main Street. There is no local significance to the name Charing Cross, which appears to derive from the monument erected in London by Edward I in memory of his wife Eleanor of Castile after her death in 1290. Rue End Street runs west from Main Street to Cathcart Street, and is one of the oldest streets in the area. Its name does not derive from *rue*, the French word for street, but instead is believed to have developed from the fact that when Greenock was still a small fishing village, this was where the fishermen's houses ended, and was referred to as the Row-end.

This view looks west from inside Scotts' Cartsburn yard over the dry dock towards the Victoria Harbour, with the East India Harbour area beyond. Construction of the Victoria Harbour was agreed in 1845 in response to pressure from local traders for provision of a tidal harbour. It was completed in 1850 at a cost of over £120,000, with debris from the excavations being used to reclaim four and a half acres of ground to form the Albert Quay further west at the Bay of Quick. A crane with a 70-ton lifting capacity was placed on the east side of the harbour, which together with the depth of water allowed some newly built vessels to be partly fitted out here. The East India Harbour had been completed in 1809 at a cost of £43,836, proving suitable for Clyde steamers and other coastal vessels such as puffers for the coaling trade to the West Highlands. In 1823 the new East India Graving Dock was added for refitting these types of vessels, and in 1870 James Lamont & Co. opened premises at the dock as ship repairers, boilermakers and engineers.

Prior to the Reformation there had been several Roman Catholic chapels in the Greenock area at various times, one of which was dedicated to St Lawrence and was thought to have been situated where Virginia Street was later formed. The name St Laurence (using a different spelling) was reintroduced in 1855 when the Revd William Gordon of St Mary's Parish Church established a new Roman Catholic church in Stanners Street. In time the original church came to be considered inadequate, and this new building, designed by Pugin & Pugin of London, was erected at a cost of £10,000 on a site at Dellingburn Street and Carnock Street. It was built of red Dumfriesshire sandstone and provided accommodation for 1,000 worshippers in a well-proportioned interior lit throughout by electricity. The new church was opened and dedicated by the Right Revd Dr Chisholm, Bishop of Aberdeen, on 3 November 1901. It was seriously damaged during the Blitz on 7 May 1941 and could not be restored. A replacement church was built at Kilmacolm Road in 1951 to designs by architects Gillespie, Kidd & Coia.

Greenock. St. Lawrence's Chapel

A school associated with St Laurence's Church was built at Stanners Street in 1857, and initially had a roll of a hundred pupils taught by one teacher and three pupil teachers. As pupil numbers increased a new building became necessary, and in 1881 the school moved to premises in Belville Street. By the early 1900s this new school had also become seriously overcrowded, and plans were drawn up to rebuild on the old Stanners Street site. Work on a new three-storey building started in March 1907, and this was opened on 3 February 1908 having cost an estimated £5,000. The new St Lawrence's School, which provided accommodation for 900 pupils, was intended for girls and infants, with boys transferring to the Belville Street premises at the age of seven. It is thought that this photograph was taken soon after the school opened in 1908 when the roll at Stanners Street was made up of 222 girls and 373 infants. The school remained in use until October 1973 when a replacement St Lawrence's Primary School opened at Ingleston Street.

PRINTED BY JOHN MITCHELL POLLOCK   Greenock Fire Brigade, 1905   PHOTO BY JOHN WALKER

Greenock's fire service dates back to 1753 when a water engine was purchased and housed in a shed in William Street which was shared with the post office. Over the years the service operated from a variety of central locations, moving in January 1887 to bespoke accommodation in the newly completed municipal buildings. Situated in the Dalrymple Street frontage of the buildings, the new premises included stables for the horses used to pull the engines (although it has been reported that the same horses were often used to tow tramcars on the local service to Gourock). In the 1930s Greenock Corporation became aware of the need for new premises to replace the congested facility underneath the town buildings, but before it could proceed the Second World War broke out. It was during this conflict, however, that the service faced one of its greatest challenges – the devastation of the Greenock Blitz of May 1941. After the war a number of years passed before a suitable site was identified at Dellingburn Street between Rue End and Carnock Streets, on ground previously occupied by the Victoria Picture House and St Laurence's Church. The new fire station (illustrated here) opened on this site on 24 June 1970.

Entitled 'Fresh Herring', this photograph shows a fish cart outside a general store at 21 Ingleston Street. Herring fishing was once a staple industry in Greenock, and the town's earliest motto was 'Let Herring Swim that Trade Maintain'. It is said that as early as 1674 20,000 barrels of herring were being exported from Greenock annually, and a few years later it was claimed that herring caught at Greenock were larger, firmer and of a better taste than those fished elsewhere. John Scott began building herring busses and other coasting vessels in 1711, and by 1778 Greenock owned 300 fishing boats, employing about 1,000 people. The subsidiary industries of fish curing and coopering took place in the Mid and West Quay areas. Herring fishing declined from the early nineteenth century when pollution from emergent industries and increasing steamboat traffic caused the fish to disappear from the Clyde. It is thought that the name Ingleston derives from the words 'English town', referring to a group of English workers who settled in Cartsdyke in 1700 to establish a bottle factory.

MUSSEL BOATS DISCHARGING, EAST INDIA HARBOUR, GREENOCK.

At one time fishing for mussels employed between forty and fifty men in the Greenock and Port Glasgow area. During its peak in the 1870s and 80s, 30,000 tons of mussels were landed at Greenock annually, earning an average of sixteen shillings a ton, and were then despatched by rail all over Scotland. In October 1888 the Scottish Mussel Bed Commission held an enquiry into the overfishing of the mussel beds on the Clyde, concluding that the quality of the remaining beds (or 'scalps') was considered to be indifferent, and that a protective fishing order should be considered for the area between Langbank and Greenock. Drummond's Cooperage (background) was established by John Drummond in 1876 when most commodities were packed in hogsheads and barrels. However, following the introduction of jute bags for sugar, and the changing requirements of commerce in general, Drummond's diversified into the manufacture of tin boxes and packing cases. A new facility was opened at Rue End Street in 1908, and included the first tin printing machinery in Scotland. Other areas of the building were employed in the production of wooden packing cases as well as the repair of barrels. In 1950 Drummond's was allocated one of the first factory spaces to be opened on the site of the former Caird's shipyard at Dalrymple Street, and continued to operate from there until its closure in the 1980s.

CUSTOM HOUSE QUAY, GREENOCK (LOOKING WEST) 1160. J.V.

Although there is no evidence of where the town's first customs office was located, it is known that Greenock became a custom house port as a branch of Port Glasgow in 1714. In 1728 annual customs receipts were £15,231, after which they remained steady for a number of years, rising to £57,336 by 1770. By 1814 receipts had reached £376,713, increasing to £455,596 13s. 3½d. in 1828. In the same year it was recorded that Greenock had 425 ships registered at the port with a total tonnage of 37,786 tons. By 1759 a lease of several rooms for a customs office had been taken in a tenement in Cathcart Street, from which the collector operated for almost twenty years. In 1778 Bailie James Gammell persuaded the customs officials to move to a new property which he had built at West Quay, but the ongoing increase in trade and revenues soon required larger premises, and in May 1817 the foundation stone of an extensive custom house and excise building was laid at the east end of the West Harbour. This elegant building (above, right), with its Grecian Doric portico facing the river, had been completed by 1818. A pier had been constructed by 1791 at the east end of the West Harbour where the custom house was built, and this became known both as Customhouse Quay and Steamboat Quay. From here passengers could sail to a variety of destinations, including the Western Isles, Liverpool, the Isle of Man, Londonderry, Belfast and Dublin. A small waiting room was opened on the east side of the quay by the steamer companies in 1852, but there were complaints that it had been designed back to front, and that passengers got soaked running round to the steamers on a wet day. The clock tower which was erected on the quay in 1868 was designed by local marine artist William Clark.

19

Around the beginning of the eighteenth century the people of Greenock, aware of the recent success of Port Glasgow as a port, began to realise the importance of adequate harbour facilities in taking advantage of the increasing trade coming to the Clyde. In both 1696 and 1700 the inhabitants of the town petitioned the Scottish parliament for financial assistance to build a harbour in Greenock, and were refused.

However, in 1707, the year that the Act of Union with England became effective, the townspeople embarked on a harbour project at their own expense. Finance was obtained via a loan from Sir John Schaw, who advanced the sum of £5,000 towards the work on condition that he be repaid by a levy of 1s. 4d. on every sack of malt brewed into ale in the town. The debt was paid off in thirty years.

When construction of the harbour commenced, the project was considered to be the greatest work of its kind then undertaken in Scotland. It was completed in 1710, and comprised East and West Quays, with a central tongue called the Mid Quay. The area, collectively known as the West Harbour, covered eight acres, and the facility had a depth of eighteen feet at high water and eight feet at low water. It allowed Greenock to take advantage of the trading opportunities arising from the Act of Union, and resulted in

a rapid increase in both foreign and coasting trade. In the first *Statistical Account of Scotland* of 1796 it was noted that Greenock merchants imported rum, sugar, cotton and mahogany from the West Indies; rice, potash, oil and timber from America; wine and fruit from southern Europe; and a considerable quantity of timber from the Baltic. Coasting trade was carried out to all the ports of Ireland, the Western Isles and the west of England, with exports of herring, coals and a variety of Scottish manufactures particularly prevalent.

By 1751 the West Harbour needed to be extended, resulting in further offices and business premises, cellars and dwelling houses being built alongside its quays. A graving dock and tar pots were added in 1784 to assist with the repair of vessels. However, by the beginning of the nineteenth century the continuing expansion of foreign trade was creating a demand for increased harbour facilities to accommodate larger vessels. The preferred option was to build another harbour to the east of the original one, resulting in the development of the East India Harbour. This, plus the later massive harbour developments which spread along the east side of the town, left the West Harbour to concentrate on providing for coasting and other small vessels, which it did until the 1920s when it began to be filled in.

As local shipping interests increased, the provision of dry dock accommodation for the repair and maintenance of vessels became a matter of growing importance for ship owners and merchants. In 1783 subscribers asked the council for ground for this purpose on the west side of the Mid Quay, and by 1784 sufficient subscriptions had been raised to build a graving dock in the westernmost division of the harbour. The work was completed by Hugh Kirkwood at a cost of £4,000 and included pumping equipment designed by James Watt. Seen here, the dock was used until the First World War, when several concrete ships were reportedly built in the facility. By August 1920 it was being filled in with debris removed as part of the work to level and extend Harland & Wolff's adjacent shipyard. To assist with the movement of the infill material a temporary narrow gauge railway was built from the shipyard to the dry dock, and for a time the small train of bogies with its toy-like locomotive was a source of great interest to passers-by.

East Breast.

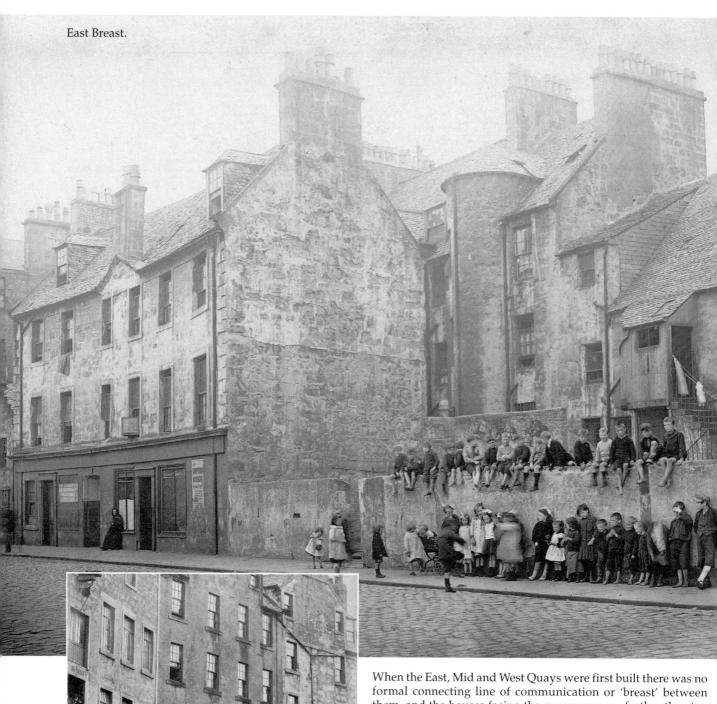

Peter Gatherer's business (centre) was located at 7 West Breast until about 1878, when the main store moved to 21–23 Crawfurd Street. J. Robertson's premises (right) were at No. 8.

When the East, Mid and West Quays were first built there was no formal connecting line of communication or 'breast' between them, and the houses facing the quays were no further than ten feet from the water's edge. The formation of the East and West Breasts was the result of later improvements, when seven feet of ground from the harbour's edge was paved, allowing improved access to cellars, businesses and houses. In 1752 the first public clock in the centre of Greenock was installed at West Breast, at the entrance to the harbour through the town cellars buildings, known as the Bell Entry. This was in use until 1839. The volume of trade at the harbour led to the establishment of shipping offices and associated businesses close to the quays. The Greenock Bank, for example, moved from its original location in Hamilton Street to premises at the West Breast beside the custom house a few years after the latter's relocation in 1778. The first major widening of the harbour breasts began in 1805 and was completed in 1819. Both East and West Breast remained a mixture of commercial premises and dwelling houses until they disappeared with the improvement scheme of 1919.

When Greenock began to develop around the harbour there were two main streets: Laigh Street, later Shaw Street (seen here from Cross Shore Street); and High Street, later Dalrymple Street. Running off these was a whole series of closes and narrow lanes such as East Quay Lane, Broad Close, Highland Close, Drummer's Close and Taylor's Close. Longwell Close – which later became Duff Street – received its name from the fifty-foot deep well which had been sunk in the area as early as 1682. Between Longwell Close and William Street was the strangely named Mince Collop Close. Within these narrow thoroughfares close to the waterfront, a haphazard maze of buildings emerged over a period of 200 years, eventually resulting in notoriously overcrowded slum housing conditions. Housing problems in Greenock were aggravated by the large influxes of people to the town seeking work during the eighteenth and early nineteenth centuries, when no real infrastructure existed to govern matters such as planning, water supply or sanitation. In 1701 the town's population stood at 746. By 1801 it had reached 17,450, and forty years later in 1841 the figure had doubled to 35,921. Over the next forty years the increases were remarkable, with the total reaching 66,704 by 1881. For much of this period a large proportion of Greenock's inhabitants were housed within the twenty acres of the central harbour area in congested and insanitary conditions, resulting in frequent outbreaks of fever, smallpox and cholera. At one point over 16,000 people in the area did not have WCs attached to their houses, and relied on the weekly collection of waste from back court receptacles. Over 66 per cent of families lived in houses of only one or two apartments, and a great many of these were sublet, with two families frequently sharing one room. The first major step in dealing with this problem was taken by the town council following the Artisans' and Labourers' Dwellings Act 1875, which gave local authorities powers of compulsory purchase of 'areas unfit for human habitation', so that they could be rebuilt and the houses let by the authorities.

Back court, 40 Shaw Street.

Back court, 48 Shaw Street.

Left: Unidentified lane showing a jib boom extending from one of the properties. These poles were joined up by rope and used as clothes lines.

In 1877 the council held an enquiry into the condition of properties in the lower part of the town from the Vennel to East Quay Lane, and between the river and Hamilton and Cathcart Streets. The buildings in this area included a considerable number of tenemental dwelling houses and shops, plus hotels, stores, cellars, stables, coal rees, cooperages and outhouses. One house inspected was described as being a single apartment, rented for 8s. 6d. per month, with its floor half-rotten and the windows so small as scarcely to allow any light to enter. In some properties people could not stand erect, water streamed down the walls, the chimney smoked and there was no water supply. As a result of the 1877 housing enquiry 605 houses reported as unfit for human habitation were demolished, and 2,700 people displaced. The old closes were swept away and East Quay Lane disappeared to be replaced by Brymner Street, while the Vennel and Dalrymple Street were widened. Many people were moved to new properties in Dempster Street and Prospecthill Street, and new tenements were built on parts of the cleared area. Further clearances were made as a result of the 1919 Greenock Improvement Order, which proposed the demolition of over 300 dwelling houses to make way for an extension to Harland & Wolff's shipyard.

Back court, West Quay Lane.

Dalrymple Street and the corner of West Quay Lane.

The north-east corner of Nicholson Street and Crawfurd Street, the western boundary of the 1919 improvement order.

These buildings in Shaw Street were finally demolished in 1923, after which the line of the street became part of Dalrymple Street. The house with the four dormer windows, at the corner of Cross Shore Street, had the date 1716 clearly carved on the stone above the central doorway. When first built its roof was thatched, but it reputedly later became one of the first houses in Greenock to have a slate roof. The building was erected by a Mr John Speir and its original use was as an inn which was the starting point for the twice-daily coach service to Glasgow. It was also believed to have been one of the earliest meeting places of the town council, which often showed a partiality to using hostelries for committee meetings. For a time there was a sundial on the corner of the building, which was used as a public timepiece prior to public clocks being erected at the Bell Entry in 1752 and in the Mid Kirk steeple in 1786.

East Quay Lane was one of the first thoroughfares to be opened up in Greenock, and eventually extended from Cathcart Street station to Customhouse Quay. By the mid-nineteenth century it was the only means of access to the waterfront for travellers arriving in Greenock by train to catch steamers for the Clyde Coast, Western Isles, Liverpool or Ireland, and even occasionally transatlantic vessels. On wet days the lane was ankle deep in mud, and muggings of steamer passengers were not uncommon, leading one to comment that it was 'a most ungracious part of Greenock'. In 1866 discussions between the council and the Caledonian Railway included a suggestion that the lane be roofed over with glass, thus creating an arcade providing both shelter and shops. This idea was never developed, however, and the pressure on passengers was eased in 1869 when Princes Pier opened, providing direct access to the steamers via its integrated station. The lane was cleared c.1878 as part of the Improvement Trust scheme chaired by Bailie Graham Brymner and replaced by Brymner Street in his honour. Now only the lower part of that street remains.

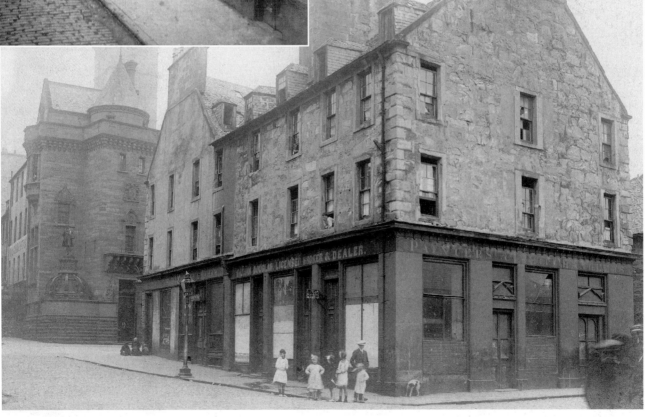

The lower end of William Street at its corner with West Breast, with the Watt Memorial School visible further up the street. A thoroughfare designed to run straight from the Mid Quayhead to the area which later became Cathcart Square was first laid out in 1751 and was known simply as New Street. At the time the upper part of the street was occupied by gardens, and was described by Lady Schaw as 'the beauty of the town'. The first feuar was William Alexander, who built a house on the east side of the street in 1752 which in its day was notable for the internal walls, which were wainscoted (wood-panelled) from head to foot. Known as the 'great tenement', the property is Greenock's oldest surviving domestic building. At a meeting on 8 August 1775 the town council considered it necessary to name streets to distinguish them from one another, and William Street was named after William Alexander. The houses in the foreground were demolished as part of the 1919 improvement order.

Without doubt the most famous native of Greenock is the engineer and inventor James Watt. He was born in 1736 in a house generally accepted to have been located at what later became the south-west corner of William Street and Dalrymple Street. This was demolished at the end of the eighteenth century and replaced by a tenement whose middle flat was occupied for many years by a hostelry known as the Greenock Tavern, later called the James Watt Inn (above). During election times this was often the headquarters of one or other of the local parties competing for municipal or parliamentary office, and in the days of limited franchise was frequently kept for weeks as an open house for voters. It was demolished c.1878 as part of the Improvement Trust operations.

James Watt became a mathematical instrument maker at the University of Glasgow in 1757. When a model of a Newcomen steam engine was brought to his workshop for repair in 1764, he identified the deficiencies in its design, and as a result developed the idea of the separate condenser. This was probably the greatest single improvement to the reciprocating steam engine, increasing its efficiency and thereby providing a major key to the progress of the Industrial Revolution.

The official opening of the Watt Memorial Engineering and Navigation School (right) took place on 1 June 1908, with the unveiling of the statue of James Watt performed by Dr Andrew Carnegie. The bronze statue had been cast by Henry Fehr of London and stood eight feet six inches high on the Dalrymple Street corner of the building. This had been designed in eighteenth century Scottish domestic style by David Barclay of Glasgow, and cost £7,000 excluding furniture and fittings. Engineering classes were to be held on the ground floor, while navigation was taught on the upper level, which provided access to the flat roof to allow students to take observations of the sun. A particular feature

of the new school was the large number of working models of passenger and cargo vessels presented by local shipbuilders Caird's and Russell's, items which were invaluable to naval architecture students. Following the opening ceremony, a lunch was served in Greenock town hall at which Andrew Carnegie proposed a toast to the 'immortal memory of James Watt'.

Taylor's Close was one of the broadest of a network of closes that existed in the centre of the town in the area now covered by the municipal buildings. Others included Drummer's Close, Mince Collop Close, Split Close and Baron Galbraith's Close. Probably named after its first feu holder, Taylor's Close ran down from Hamilton Street to Dalrymple Street, passing the west side of the old town house. This had been built in 1766 behind the town offices, and was separated from them by a narrow street which later became the covered carriageway to the present town hall. By the mid-nineteenth century the town house was considered too small, and was reconstructed in 1858 at a cost of £1,700 with a higher roof and accommodation for over 2,000 people. It was a further twenty years before plans were made to demolish the old council offices and replace them with new municipal buildings. At the same time the opportunity arose to sweep away some of the slums in the area, and Taylor's Close disappeared in the 1880s as part of this programme. The presence of the policemen in the photographs is explained by the fact that the old police offices stood on the east side of the close (above). These were built about 1850 and designed by the master of works William Allison, who later designed the town hall in 1858. By 1880 the offices were becoming crowded, and as cell accommodation had been condemned as unsuitable by a government inspector, the opportunity was taken to transfer the police into new offices in the Dalrymple Street side of the municipal buildings.

West side of Taylor's Close.

With the construction of the municipal buildings, the area formerly occupied by Taylor's Close became known as Wallace Place (illustrated here). It is not clear whether this was named after Robert Wallace, Greenock's first MP, or (more likely) Dr James Wallace, a medical officer on the parochial board for twenty-five years who was very active in campaigning to rid Greenock of its slum areas. The building on the left, now housing offices, was used from 1882–99 as Greenock's general post office. Prior to this the post office had several homes including premises within the custom house, at Watt Place and at 1 Church Place. In 1899 it moved to commodious new premises in Cathcart Street on the site of the original Tontine Hotel. Meanwhile, the Public Libraries (Scotland) Act was adopted by the town council in 1900, and the following year the former post office building was purchased from the Improvement Trust as premises for a free public library, with financial assistance of £8,000 from Andrew Carnegie. Greenock's Central Library remained here until 1970 when it moved to new premises in Clyde Square.

This photograph was taken from Hunter Place in May 1923 following the clearance of property in the lower Vennel. Plans for the new municipal buildings were approved at a special council meeting in August 1877. For thirty years previously the council had looked for a suitable location, and when it decided to remain on the existing town offices site in Hamilton Street it began to buy up surrounding land for the project. A competition for the design of the buildings was announced, attracting over eighty entries. The winning one – by Hugh & David Barclay on the theme 'Art and Science' – was unanimously approved at an estimated cost of £80,000, plus £60,000 for the site. The foundation stone was laid on 6 August 1881 in one of the piers of the Victoria Tower, and the first section to be built was the Dalrymple Street elevation. By 1884 there was a motion to delay the third section, which included the collecting hall, on financial grounds. However, work continued despite criticism that 'every beauty but the beauty of economy had been studied in the erection of the municipal buildings', and by 1888 they were completed at a final cost of £200,000.

Lindsay Lane was near the dry dock, and ran behind West Breast between the Vennel and West Quay Lane, parallel to Dalrymple Street. It had been named in the mid-eighteenth century after Joseph Lindsay, master of the vessel *Schaw* of Greenock. In the 1790s the area between Mid Quay and West Quay was largely occupied by herring barrels, often to the exclusion of other goods, resulting in occasional complaints from other traders against the fish curers. At that time only the south side of Lindsay Lane had been built up and the houses fronted the harbour, and as a result of the congestion on the quayside the magistrates were obliged to pass an order restricting the herring trade to the area of the lane. In time this space proved insufficient, and gradually the trade began to extend into a new street called Herring Street (later Charles Street). The cooperages were spread over this area, and the din of heading and hooping barrels was heard continuously from morning till night during the fishing season. Lindsay Lane was swept away around May 1921.

Ropework Street ran west from Dalrymple Street at Westburn Square to Laird Street, curving round between the back of the Old West Kirk and Caird's shipyard. It was named after the extensive ropework in the area which had originated *c.*1725, and which was reckoned to be one of the oldest industrial firms in Greenock. Its first partners were the Bogle family of Glasgow, West India merchants who brought their ships to Greenock. By 1776 the works were being operated by John Laird and his sons Alexander and William, who remained in charge until 1820 when the firm was dissolved. Some members of the Laird family moved to Liverpool, establishing a shipbuilding yard at Birkenhead. Later, the ropework building was purchased by the town council and used at various times as a poorhouse, ragged school, mission Sunday school and cholera hospital, until it was demolished in 1867 during the construction of the Albert Harbour. The remainder of Ropework Street disappeared during the 1920s extensions to Harland & Wolff's shipyard. This picture shows the Highland Mary tavern, which featured a portrait of Mary Campbell on its lamp, a reference to the fact that Burns's Highland Mary was buried in the nearby churchyard of the Old West Kirk. **31**

In 1589 James VI granted John Schaw of Greenock a charter to build a church and manse and open a graveyard for the people who lived on his lands. As a result the Old West Kirk (as it was later known) was completed in 1591, serving a parish that stretched from Inverkip to Kilmacolm. The church was located beside the Clyde, close to the mouth of the West Burn, and around this landmark a more settled population developed slowly into the community of Greenock. The original building underwent various enlargements and alterations over the years. At one point it became so decayed that it closed in 1841 for over twenty years, during which time the graveyard was so greatly neglected that it became a public nuisance. However, in 1863 a decision was taken to

restore the historic church, and it reopened on 25 December 1864. The repairs cost £2,400, over half of which was raised by public subscription. Caird's shipbuilding yard had been established beside the church in 1844, and in 1917 new owners Harland & Wolff first put forward proposals for a huge extension to the shipyard which involved incorporation of the church site shown in the photograph. Following years of negotiation and considerable opposition to the moving of the graveyard in particular, Harland & Wolff undertook to dismantle and rebuild the church at Seafield on the Esplanade. It closed in 1925 and reopened on its new site in February 1928. A plaque on Container Way opposite Tesco's store marks its original location.

In August 1931 an enquiry was held into housing conditions in the central area of Greenock comprising Church Place, Sir Michael Street, Market Street, Manse Lane, Cowgate and the Vennel. Some of the houses in this small area were thought to be 175 years old. The Vennel (meaning narrow lane or passage), which ran from the old West Quay to Inverkip Street, was one of the oldest streets in Greenock, and had developed after the construction of the West Harbour in 1707. It was originally quite a respectable centre of civic life, with many merchants and ship owners living there. In 1760 Lady Schaw described it as a very handsome street, surpassed only by the recently opened William Street. However, rapid population growth throughout the nineteenth century led to urgent demands for housing, and properties in the Vennel area deteriorated due to subdividing, backland development, and the effects of serious overcrowding and poor property maintenance. As illustrated elsewhere, parts of the lower Vennel were cleared under improvement schemes in 1877 and 1919, while a 1931 compulsory purchase order sought to tackle the area south of Hamilton Street. The enquiry heard that 3,205 people lived in the area in 700 houses, where the majority of rents were £10 a year or under. 85 per cent of dwellings were either one- or two-apartment, resulting in severe overcrowding. The houses were showing the effects of age and were in considerable disrepair. Many windows could not be opened, ceilings were low and sagging, and in a large number of houses there was bug and rat infestation. The majority of staircases, internal walls and floors were wooden and not fireproof, while on the other hand many properties were below street level and suffered considerable dampness. There was a lack of natural ventilation and sunlight; very few houses had sculleries or cupboards in which to store food; only two had baths and none had hot water. A survey had shown that on average there was one WC – usually situated in the back court area – for every eighteen people. There were limited facilities for washing clothes, with only thirteen wash-houses available, some of which had no tubs, leaving no alternative to washing and drying clothes in the houses. Despite these circumstances, many people fought to maintain a high standard of cleanliness, and resented the use of the word slum to describe their homes. The dilapidation of the area was largely caused by structural deterioration, lack of repair, poor sanitation and narrow streets. Given the cramped conditions, together with the Scottish tradition of recess and concealed beds, it was not surprising that the area recorded higher than average statistics for diseases and infant mortality. The death rates from tuberculosis, non-pulmonary tuberculosis and respiratory diseases were all double the average for the town. Despite the objections of some property owners, clearance of the area began almost immediately after Greenock Corporation was granted the necessary compulsory purchase order in 1931 and continued throughout the 1930s. Subsequent redevelopment led to the disappearance of streets such as Market Street and Cowgate, and the creation of a new thoroughfare of High Street along the approximate line of the Vennel. This picture shows Market Street in 1908.

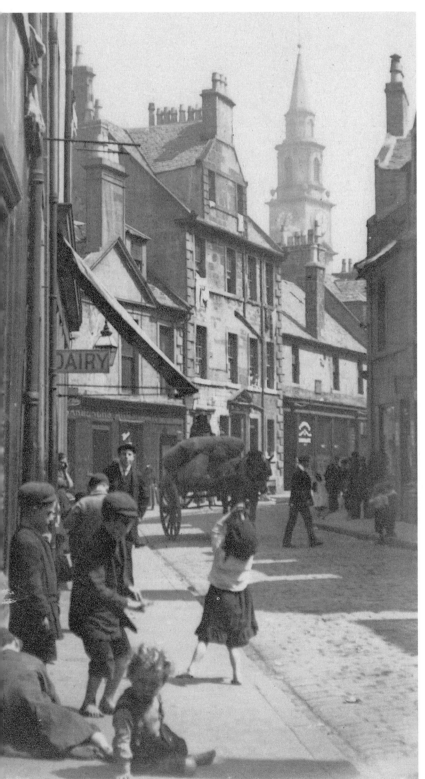

Nos. 16 and 18 Market Street.

Vennel looking north-east from Inverkip Street.

Manse Lane looking southwards from Hamilton Street.

No. 7 Market Street.

Sir Michael Street looking
southwards from the Vennel.

Sugarhouse Lane looking
northwards from the Vennel.

WAVERLEY LANE
WILLIAM LOUDON.
WHOLESALE PROVISION MERCHANT.

Waverley Lane from Westburn Street.

Following public agitation in favour of introducing a railway to Greenock, a meeting in the town hall in December 1835 resolved to form a joint-stock company to facilitate the formation of a line between Glasgow, Paisley and Greenock. This opened on 30 March 1841 having cost £814,000. The original estimate was for £400,000 but in building the line many natural obstacles had to be overcome. The first station at Greenock (below) was at the end of Cathcart Street near Customhouse Quay, allowing steamer connections to be introduced at an early date. On the first day of service 300 passengers left Greenock for Glasgow in twelve carriages drawn by two locomotives. The journey took 65 minutes. The return journey left Glasgow at 1.30 p.m. and arrived back in Greenock at 2.50 p.m. Within a short period of time the railway was transporting 2,000 passengers a day.

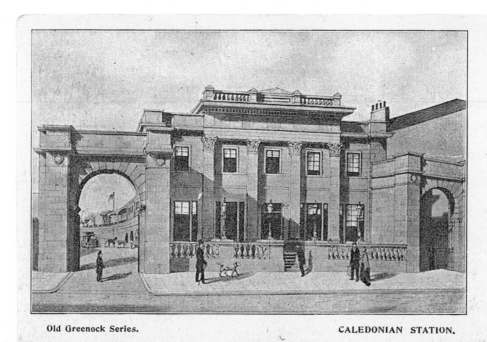

Old Greenock Series.   CALEDONIAN STATION.

Cathcart Street was originally a turnpike road eighteen feet broad, and first began to be feued in 1758. In August 1775 it was one of the first streets to be officially named by the town council, in this case after the Cathcart family who were first associated with Greenock in 1718 through the marriage of Charles, 8th Baron Cathcart to Marion Schaw. The street developed very much as the commercial centre of the town, and housed coffee rooms, the sugar exchange, the assembly rooms, the *Greenock Advertiser* newspaper office and several banks. The original Tontine Hotel was situated in Cathcart Street and provided thirty bedrooms, twelve sitting rooms and a large hall. In 1892 the site was sold to the government for a main post office building, and the Tontine moved to the premises in Union Street from which it still operates.

As trade increased in Greenock throughout the eighteenth century the need for local banking facilities became essential. Until 1785 banking business was conducted in Glasgow, and all transactions had to be sent to the city by stagecoach, or in an emergency by express horseback. The Greenock Bank was the first bank to be opened in the town and originally

Overleaf: On the night of 6 May 1941, Greenock suffered bombing for a period of two hours from about 50 enemy planes. During this raid several residential properties situated throughout the town were severely damaged, resulting in a considerable number of civilian casualties. The following night brought an even greater attack, when it was estimated that between 250 and 300 German aircraft took part in the raid in three waves. A large number of incendiary bombs and high explosives were dropped in the first two raids, while just after 2 a.m. a third raid of high explosives and parachute landmines caused heavy damage throughout a widespread area. By 3.30 a.m. the whole town between James Watt Dock and Cathcart Square appeared to be ablaze, and fire brigade units were rushed from throughout the west

operated from premises in Hamilton Street, although by 1818 it had moved to 44 Cathcart Street, while the Glasgow Union Bank was at No. 74. Over the years the street housed many banks including the Commercial at the corner of Cross Shore Street, and by 1836 the Royal Bank of Scotland had been established at 8 Cathcart Street.

of Scotland to assist the local services extinguish the huge fires. Meanwhile police and ARP (air-raid precaution) personnel were involved in rescuing many people trapped in shelters, tenements and industrial premises. In total over the two nights 280 people were killed and over 1,200 were injured. 10,000 houses suffered some form of damage, including 1,000 which were destroyed. Several industrial premises were extensively damaged, including the Westburn and Walker's sugar refineries; Dellingburn power station; Rankin & Blackmore's foundry; Lamont's dry dock and Scotts' head office. The following photographs show some of the damage caused in Cathcart Street and nearby Dalrymple Street, recorded on 8 May 1941 by James Hall, official war photographer for the area.

Cathcart Street looking west towards the Mid Kirk.

Cathcart Street at the corner of Duff Street.

Cathcart Street at the corner of Broad Close.

Dalrymple Street looking east from Brymner Street.

Horse-drawn trams were first introduced to Greenock on 7 July 1873, running from the east end of Cathcart Street to the Gourock boundary. By 1883 there was a service leaving Greenock every fifteen minutes, those on the hour and half-hour to Ashton, on the quarter hours to Cardwell Bay. In 1889 the service was extended to Port Glasgow. The Greenock & Port Glasgow Tramway Company obtained powers to adapt the whole line to electric running in 1898, and electric trams were introduced for public use on 3 October 1901. The service reached a peak in 1918 with almost seventeen million passenger journeys per annum, but thereafter business suffered a downturn due to depression in trade, widespread unemployment and increased competition from motor buses, whose greater mobility was an advantage in the area's hilly topography. This photograph shows Greenock's last tramcar in Cathcart Square with Provost John Drummond at the helm, on the final day's service on 15 July 1929. Behind the tram is one of the 'new, spacious and luxurious' motor buses which had first been introduced in 1924.

Opposite: Known simply as 'The Square' for many years, Cathcart Square was formed before 1751 and was later named after the Cathcart family's connection with the town (see p40). In 1761 the Mid Kirk was built on the south side of the square, and by 1770 the White Hart Hotel was to be found on the north-east corner. In the nineteenth century it became a favourite haunt of town councillors, and it has been said that meetings were frequently held in the White Hart to revise minutes and discuss the filling of vacancies. As noted on page 29, Greenock's first town house had been built in 1766 behind the council offices, but by the 1850s it was considered to be too small and there was a general desire for a larger building to match Glasgow City Hall. As a result today's town hall was rebuilt in 1858 on the town house site, and its front elevation can be seen in the middle of this picture before it was surrounded by the addition of the municipal buildings. To obtain the appropriate site for the proposed new municipal buildings, the town council began buying up land surrounding the town hall from the 1870s onwards. However, it was unsuccessful in acquiring the property on the south-west corner of Cathcart Square owned by Robert Cowan (advertising the *Weekly Herald* in this photograph). Cowan was not prepared to sell his site below his own price, but his gamble failed and the construction of the municipal buildings proceeded around his property without the inclusion of 'Cowan's Corner'.

This view looks west from Cathcart Square towards Hamilton Street, which at one time was the back limit of the town. In the left foreground is the portico of the Mid Kirk, which was built to meet the needs of a growing population for a second place of worship in the town. In 1758 Lord Cathcart gave ground in the square for the building of a church for the new or middle parish. It was constructed using stone from a quarry in Newton Street and the seating arrangements for 1,600 worshippers were planned by James Watt's father. The design of the portico was based on St Martin-in-the-Fields, London, and the steeple was added in 1786. On the right-hand side of the picture is David Coltart's drapery, which was built on the site of Robert Cowan's property. In the Blitz of May 1941 the property at Cowan's Corner suffered such extensive bomb damage that it had to be demolished. Eventually the town council was able to acquire the site, and in recent years used the ground as a seating area and garden designed for the blind and partially sighted.

Situated next to the Union Bank at 3 Hamilton Street was an ice cream saloon and confectioner's shop operated by the Landi brothers, whose home address was also here. The business operated from about 1913 until 1933. Occupying the same building from about 1900 was the firm of D. Kirk, slater, which continued to trade from the premises until their demolition in the 1930s, by which time Kirk's also had premises at 23 Inverkip Street. The Hamilton Street building was included in the 1931 central area clearance proposals, and one distinct improvement put forward for the area opposite the municipal buildings was the formation of an open square and gardens, later named Clyde Square.

Hamilton Street was one of the first streets to be formally laid out in the town, and was originally designated in 1759 'to run from the Square to the Long Vennel'. This designation was later revised 'to run from the Square to the Kirk Burn, i.e. the West Burn'. The first feus were taken on the south side of the street before the council built its town house on the opposite side in 1766 on the site of the present municipal buildings. A number of the premises opposite the municipal buildings (whose front elevation can be seen on the right of this picture) were demolished in the central clearances of the 1930s. However, it was not until the 1950s that Clyde Square was laid out as an open space with gardens. This disappeared again in the late 1960s with the construction of the Central Library during the first phase of the new town centre development. The presence of both a bus and a tram in this picture dates it to between 1924 and 1929.

In 1960 Greenock Corporation took the first steps towards redevelopment of the town centre area when it approved a set of design proposals drawn up by the Murrayfield Real Estate Company. At the time it was stated that although there were some very good shops along Hamilton Street at ground level, and several medium sized stores which extended to some depth, there were no buildings in the area of any great value or architectural merit, with the exception of the municipal buildings and the Mid Kirk. In order to consider all the possibilities available for the site, a scheme was drawn up allowing the complete redevelopment of the whole area bounded by Dalrymple Street, Westburn Street, High Street, Cathcart Street and William Street. The 1960 plan comprised a scheme providing 600 houses and 150 shops. Among the buildings to go would be the corporation shops and houses of fairly recent date on High Street, the new electricity showroom, the bank building on Hamilton Street, Martyrs and North Church, the public library and the *Greenock Telegraph* offices. In addition, the newly completed double carriageway at High Street would disappear and the green belt of Clyde Square would be redesigned. The original proposals had five criteria:

1. The separation of vehicular and pedestrian traffic circulation, with the shopping precinct to become completely pedestrianised except for car parking and servicing

2. Provision of adequate servicing for all shops and commercial premises
3. Provision of large numbers of houses in the form of six blocks of multi-storey flats
4. Enhancement of the existing civic centre
5. Careful consideration to landscaping and civic amenities both within and adjoining the precinct

With regard to planning, the redevelopment would be carried out in several distinct stages to reduce disturbance and hardship. It was suggested that there should probably be six phases taking three to five years to complete, and that the first phase should be the north side of Hamilton Street. In the shopping arcade there would be standard shopping units which could be let in multiples, and several large stores of three-storey height. Canopies would be provided along the shopfronts to offer weather protection. In the event the Murrayfield scheme was cancelled, but in 1968 the council finally started a town centre development programme covering much of the area described in the original proposals. The first phase began at Clyde Square with the construction of the Central Library, and developed westwards over a number of years, resulting in major changes to the appearance of central Greenock, and the disappearance of several streets such as Charles Street, Sugarhouse Lane, Westburn Square and Waverley Lane.

Clyde Square photographed from Shaw Place, 1968.

King St

The High Street, King Street and Smith Street area in 1965, seen from the Mid Kirk.

High Street looking north from Crown Street.

High Street looking west from Smith Street.

Smith Street looking south from High Street at the South of Scotland Electricity Board's showroom.

High Street looking east from the roundabout, 1970. Sugarhouse Lane is first on the left, followed by Charles Street.

High Street roundabout from Inverkip Street, with the junction of Westburn Street on the left.

Hamilton Street looking east from Charles Street.

The north side of Hamilton Street between Charles Street and Sugarhouse Lane.

The east side of Westburn Street photographed from Kilblain Street, 1969.

The south side of Hamilton Street looking up Sugarhouse Lane, 1970.

The glazing firm of Briton & Baillie was established at 26 Sugarhouse Lane in 1871. Within a short time William Baillie had left the business and Thomas Briton had moved to premises at No. 19. By 1899 the business had expanded to include artists' materials, picture framing, carving and gilding, and operated as such until its closure c.1908. The first recorded sugar refinery in Greenock was built in 1765 in response to the growing import of cane sugar to the Clyde from the West Indies. It was located close to the West Burn at the foot of the street which became known as Sugarhouse Lane. In 1788 a second refinery was opened at the other end of the lane by a syndicate of local citizens, one of whom was Robert Macfie. His son later operated the Bogle Street refinery. By 1872 there were fourteen refineries in the town, producing about a quarter of a million tons of sugar annually, but competition, foreign trade barriers and the arrival of beet sugar to Britain caused a slump towards the end of the nineteenth century. By the end of the First World War the situation had recovered, and Greenock remained a major source of refined cane sugar and syrup, with its two remaining refineries latterly producing more than the earlier fourteen. Walker's refinery closed in 1979 and the Westburn ceased operating in 1997, bringing over 230 years of sugar refining in Greenock to an end.

West Blackhall Street runs westwards from the end of the covered Oak Mall at Westburn Street, named after the West Burn, which at one time flowed openly through the town centre and required the building of a number of bridges to allow townspeople to cross it safely. The house on the right was where the novelist John Galt died in April 1839. Although born in Irvine, he lived in Greenock for fifteen years as a young man, and worked as a clerk in the custom house. He left Greenock in 1804 and for a time led a fairly adventurous life of travel in Europe and Canada. However, on his return to Britain in 1829 he spent several months in a debtors' prison, and on his release settled back in Greenock to continue writing. He is best remembered for his Scottish novels *The Ayrshire Legatees*, *Annals of the Parish* and *The Provost*. This view shows West Blackhall Street (looking west) at the junction with Westburn Street.

West Blackhall Street (seen here looking west from the corner of Nicholson Street) began to expand in the 1850s and grew to include a wide-ranging mix of shops and offices, dwelling houses, closes and pends. It developed a reputation as the principal area for quality shopping in the town, but remained outwith the 1960s proposals for redevelopment of the town centre. Whilst the general line of the street has remained the same, over the years there have been many demolitions and replacements of individual properties, plus changes to shop frontages and types of businesses. Together with the renumbering of properties, this can make exact comparisons with present-day buildings difficult.

The long-established firm of Shannons was founded in 1870 by James Shannon as the Greenock Clothing Company, and over the years occupied several premises in the town. The original shop was in Cathcart Street in the building known as the Arcade, but in 1878 the company moved to the White Hart Hotel building at the north-east corner of Cathcart Square, on the site later occupied by the Clydesdale Bank. Following demolition of this building, Shannons moved to Duff Street, but by this time retail business was generally moving westwards along the town, and the firm relocated to premises at the corner of Hamilton Street and Sugarhouse Lane where they set up their main tailoring and outfitters department. Additional premises for a hat and hosiery department for men were also acquired at 11 West Blackhall Street at the corner of Nicholson Street, and in time this became the main shop. The West Blackhall Street shop was damaged in the Blitz of 1941, and ten years later in 1951 the new frontage shown here – which was to become a familiar landmark until the business closed in the late 1970s – was completed.

Havelock Buildings were erected c.1860 at the corner of West Blackhall Street and the east side of Argyle Street as a mixture of flats and commercial premises. One of the long-established businesses occupying the property from 1863 was James Black, bookseller, stationer and librarian, at No. 17 West Blackhall Street. His business was also used as a forwarding office for parcels to be carried on the Caledonian Railway. Black's disappears from trades directories in 1906 when its proprietor appears to have retired. About the same time R. G. Duthie, hairdresser and tobacconist, moved from 17 to 16 West Blackhall Street, before settling at 3 Argyle Street c.1925.

Ivie Scott is first recorded in trades directories as a grocer at 5 West Blackhall Street in 1845. As the street developed further west the firm moved to No. 20, remaining there until 1894 when it moved to 31 Brougham Street. During the same period, Ivie Scott is also listed as a grocer and provision merchant and proprietor of the branch post office at 72 Eldon Street. Next door to Scott's was Robert Climie, cutler and gunsmith, who was still at this location in the late 1930s, by then described as a cutler only. The proprietor of the Argyll Bar was Alexander McNiven, while J. & A. Miller was a firm of joiners and builders. These buildings were on the north side of West Blackhall Street, between Argyle and Jamaica Streets.

Mackay the bakers first appears in Greenock directories in 1861 at 15 West Blackhall Street, within Havelock Buildings. By 1880 the business had moved to 21 (later 71) West Blackhall Street. In 1900 these premises were taken over by a relative, Thomas Mackay, as an extension to his bakery business in Largs, with a further shop being opened at Kempock Place in Gourock. The firm became well known for its high quality bread, tea bread, cakes, shortbread and wedding cakes, many of which gained international awards. In 1923 Mackay's considered their existing premises to be too restricted, and unveiled plans for modernisation and expansion of the property. The proposals, which were completed in 1925, included remodelling the ground floor to provide ample space for the shop and offices. A stairway from within the shop (as well as an independent external stairway) led to the first floor dining room and tea room, whilst on the second floor a commodious hall suitable for suppers and dances was provided, with lounges and resting rooms adjacent. This was known as The Lorne, and was renowned for the quality of its patent sprung dance floor. Mackay's was bought by Ravenstone Securities in 1973, and closed on 25 April that year.

Entries for Mrs M. Ebbutt, costumier of 37 West Blackhall Street, appear in local trades directories between 1924 and 1931. Also located at 37–39 West Blackhall Street were Kidd Bros., described in their advertisements as removal contractors, cabinetmakers, upholsterers and carpet warehousemen. The firm had moved to this address from 6 Grey Place in 1896, and remained there until the 1940s, when the address changed to West Stewart Street and 16–18 Grey Place.

Opposite upper: For many Greenockians, one of the most fondly remembered cinemas in the town was the Central picture house at 34 West Blackhall Street. It was better known as the 'Ranch' due to the popular perception that a very high percentage of films shown there were westerns – although James Morton, manager at the cinema for many years, often maintained that statistically this was not the case. The Central opened at Christmas 1916 showing silent films, the first to be screened being *The Victim* and *Father Three and Others*. An unusual and well-appreciated feature of the cinema was the large coal fire in the foyer. The Central closed on Saturday 5 April 1958 during a period when cinema audiences were declining nationally. The last films to be shown were *The Counterfeit Plan* and *Secret File*.

Opposite lower: The Hippodrome Theatre at 40 West Blackhall Street was built in 1858 by Edward Glover as the Theatre Royal to replace an older theatre in Mansionhouse Lane. It opened on 27 December that year with a production of Shakespeare's *Much Ado About Nothing*. Until the opening of the Alexandra Theatre (later the King's) in 1905, the Theatre Royal was the home of the best drama and opera productions in the town, and many great actors of the late nineteenth century appeared on its stage. In 1908 its name was changed to the Hippodrome Theatre of Varieties, and it continued to operate as a music hall until its closure on 1 December 1923. At that time the town council planned to demolish the building and surrounding properties to facilitate a realignment of Dalrymple Street into Grey Place. It was 1930, however, before the road scheme was completed, and the last remaining walls and hoardings of the theatre were demolished in May of that year. In 1924 the three classical statues which decorated the front of the Hippodrome were relocated in Auchmountain Glen.

A CORNER OF OUR SHOWROOM
HECTOR RUSSELL (Highland Industries) LTD., 120-126 West Blackhall St., GREENOCK, Scotland

Hector Russell & Co. were originally electrical engineers who moved c.1937 to Radio House, 32 West Blackhall Street (later renumbered 120). Prior to this the business had been located at Radio Corner at 19 Hamilton Street, with a branch at 18 Cathcart Street. Hector G. Russell was listed in local trades directories from 1925 as a wireless appliance manufacturer, and appeared to open his first shops about 1930. By 1955 he was described as a radio and television dealer and the business had expanded at the West Blackhall Street address to include Highland Industries, which advertised as bagpipe makers, kiltmakers and suppliers of pipe band accessories. Shortly after this the electrical business disappeared from the directory, leaving Hector Russell Highland Industries trading from West Blackhall Street until about 1982, when part of the premises became occupied by Inverclyde Solicitors Property Centre.

This view looks east from Patrick Street along Grey Place and shows the Hippodrome Theatre before the realignment of Dalrymple Street. The domed building was the King's Theatre, built in 1905 as the Alexandra at what was then the corner of West Blackhall Street and Ker Street. Over the years it attracted many famous stage companies including the Royal Carl Rosa Company and George Edwards and his company in *The Merry Widow*. The King's converted to a cinema in 1928 and continued to operate until 1969, by which time it had become part of the Odeon chain. It was demolished in 1973. On the left is the former St Columba's Gaelic Parish Church, built in 1823. It was originally known as the West Chapel or North Church and its congregation worshipped here until 1843 when the building closed. For a number of years it was apparently used as a music hall, but in 1854 it was taken over by the congregation of St Thomas's Free Church, which used it until uniting with the Middle UF Church in 1907. At that time the congregation of St Columba's Gaelic, which had occupied several temporary premises over the years, took over the building, remaining there until 1979 when a declining roll and the need for extensive repairs led to the church's closure. St Columba's then united with the North Church to become the Old West Kirk.

The origins of St Mary's Church date back to 1802 when Roman Catholicism was re-established in Greenock. Early services were held in the Star Hall in Broad Close until 1816, when the first St Mary's was erected in East Shaw Street. As the congregation expanded, a site for a new building was acquired at the corner of Patrick Street and Brougham Street. The church was designed in early French Gothic style by George Goldie of London, and opened on 17 August 1862 with the Right Revd Dr Murdoch, Bishop of the Western District, officiating. A major renovation programme was completed in 2003. In 1909 the associated St Mary's School was built behind the church in Houston Street at a cost of £10,000. It was intended to accommodate 500 elementary and 200 secondary pupils, and was designed by Walter Wilson of Glasgow. Internally, bright, well-lit classrooms occupied three floors, while the ground floor was largely occupied by an assembly hall, plus classes for technical instruction.

George Square Congregational Church (foreground) was designed by John Baird and opened on 6 September 1840. Congregationalism in Greenock dates back to the visits of itinerant preachers to Inverkip at the end of the eighteenth century. By 1805 there were sufficient members of the church for a Congregational chapel to be built in Sir Michael Street, where the first settled preacher was John Hercus. When the growth of the congregation led to the need for a new building, a member of the church, Thomas Hamlin, merchant and ship owner, donated a site at George Square. Its congregation is now part of the United Reformed Church. Behind the square (laid out in 1789 as Kilblain Square) is the steeple of the Episcopal Church of St John the Evangelist, built in 1877 in English Gothic style to designs by Paley & Austin of Lancaster. Its tower was paid for by Sir Michael Shaw Stewart. Made of freestone from Inverkip quarry, the church replaced a former Episcopal church on the site which had opened in 1824 with accommodation for 400 sitters.

In 1818 the council commissioned David Reid to plan a new town layout from the West Burn to the Battery, resulting in the formation of the 'West End' grid of wide, straight streets. Running west from George Square, Union Street was one of the earliest of these to be developed, and by the 1840s the West End had taken on its recognisable shape. One of the few houses which predated Reid's plan was built in 1808 and was the home of George Robertson, a local merchant and magistrate. In 1892 the property (partly visible on the left) was acquired by hotel proprietor Mrs Buchanan, who converted it into replacement premises for the old Tontine Hotel in Cathcart Street. In the distance, the 200-foot spire of St George's North Church dominates

the skyline. Its congregation dates back to the Disruption of 1843 when members of the Mid Kirk left to form the Free Middle Church. They obtained ground in Westburn Street and quickly built what became known as the 'Brick Kirk'. However, problems relating to drainage at the burn led to the need for a new building, and in 1877 the Middle United Free Church, designed by Salmon, Son & Ritchie, opened at a cost of £18,863. In 1907 the congregation united with St Thomas's Church, and in 1929, having entered union with the Church of Scotland, it became St George's Church.

This view from Ardgowan Bowling Club looks towards the Scots-renaissance style building of the 'new' Mansion House on Union Street. Designed by Sir Robert Rowand Anderson, it was built in 1886 as estate offices for the Shaw Stewarts to replace the original Mansion House at Well Park (see p94) when this was demolished to make way for the Caledonian Railway's line extension from Greenock to Gourock. The land at Ardgowan Square was granted by Sir Michael Shaw Stewart in 1841 to a committee of local residents to promote the activities of bowling, curling and quoiting. A bowling green and curling pond were laid out, and 140 square feet of ground were made available for quoiting. A particular feature of the project was the paths which were laid out throughout the grounds

allowing walks of up to a mile through shrubs and flower beds. By 1863 the curling pond had been filled in and quoiting had been given up. A second bowling green and tennis courts were added to the club.

Despite some controversy over the choice of site, the Sheriff Courthouse in Nelson Street (seen here with the West Kirk beyond it) was opened in 1869 to replace an existing court-house and prison in Bank Street. At the time many people, including the local legal fraternity, considered the location to be too far west. However, the building went ahead anyway. **62** It was designed in Scots baronial style by architects Peddie &

Kinnear of Edinburgh and a particular feature was the tower and spire in the centre, which rose to 130 feet in height. Immediately behind the courthouse was the prison, containing 60 single cells plus sick cells and accommodation for punishment. This was used until 1910 when Gateside prison opened at Old Inverkip Road. In 1936 the old Nelson Street prison was demolished and the site acquired by John Hastie & Co.

In 1837 the original West Kirk at the West Burn (p32) had reached such a state of disrepair, and was considered so unwholesome and uncomfortable, that proposals for a new church were submitted to the Presbytery. After some debate and delay, a site in Nelson Street was agreed upon in April 1839 for a new building to accommodate 1,400 worshippers. Along with the minister, Dr Patrick Macfarlan, the congregation moved to the 'new' West Church on 16 May 1841. Two years later, at the Disruption of 1843, Dr Macfarlan opted for the Free Church and was replaced by Revd Dr James McCulloch, author of *McCulloch's Course of Reading*, the most notable school book of its time. Dr McCulloch was minister

The West Kirk.   Greenock.

of the West Kirk for forty years, and is commemorated by 'McCulloch's Clock', the name by which the church clock became popularly known. This was donated to the church in 1856 by Miss Francis Ann Wood, sister of Sir Gabriel Wood of the Mariners' Asylum. The West Kirk is now called St Luke's.

ARDGOWAN SCHOOL GREENOCK.

At the official opening of Ardgowan School in Nelson Street on 29 April 1898, the chairman of the school board, Dr Philip, explained that it had been built to replace three substandard schools including temporary buildings at Ann Street and Duncan Street. It also included new accommodation for deaf pupils who had previously attended the Glebe School. Dr Philip thought the school had a pleasing character externally and was one of the best of the board's schools. There was accommodation for 1,000 scholars in large, airy and well-lit classrooms, and everything had been designed to 'conduce to the well-being of the children'. As the school was located near to Inverkip Road which led to Ardgowan House, the board thought that Ardgowan would be a suitable name for it. The building continued to be used as a primary school until 1979, when pupils were moved to the former Finnart School at Newton Street. It was demolished some years later and is now the site of Ardgowan Medical Practice.

The railway line to Princes Pier (originally called Albert Harbour) was opened to the west of the new Albert Harbour facility by the Greenock & Ayrshire Railway in 1869. The line ran from St Enoch's in Glasgow to Greenock via Kilmacolm, Port Glasgow and Lynedoch Street, before reaching the pier through a long, steep tunnel. It provided a railhead further west than the Caledonian Railway's connection to Steamboat Quay and was quickly taken over by the Glasgow & South Western Railway, creating strong competition in the provision of steamer services. In due course the G&SWR began operating its own fleet of steamers to rival those of the Caledonian Steam Packet Company, and to complement these set about improving facilities at Princes Pier. As a result a new and larger station building (above) was opened on 25 May 1894 when a special train of VIPs arrived from Glasgow St Enoch's to inspect the magnificent facilities. The wide facade of the station was dominated by six Italianate towers of red Ruabon bricks, while access to the trains on the upper level was gained by two carriageways, flights of stairs and luggage lifts connecting the platforms to the pier. The lower picture shows the news-stand in the refurbished station, which was located opposite the large booking office.

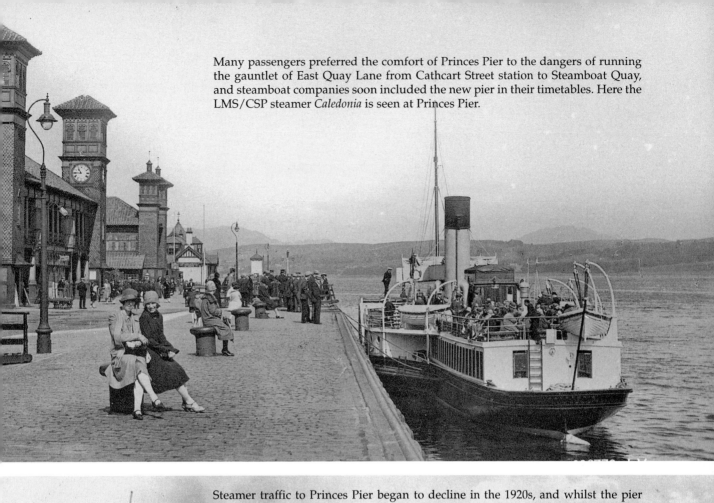

Many passengers preferred the comfort of Princes Pier to the dangers of running the gauntlet of East Quay Lane from Cathcart Street station to Steamboat Quay, and steamboat companies soon included the new pier in their timetables. Here the LMS/CSP steamer *Caledonia* is seen at Princes Pier.

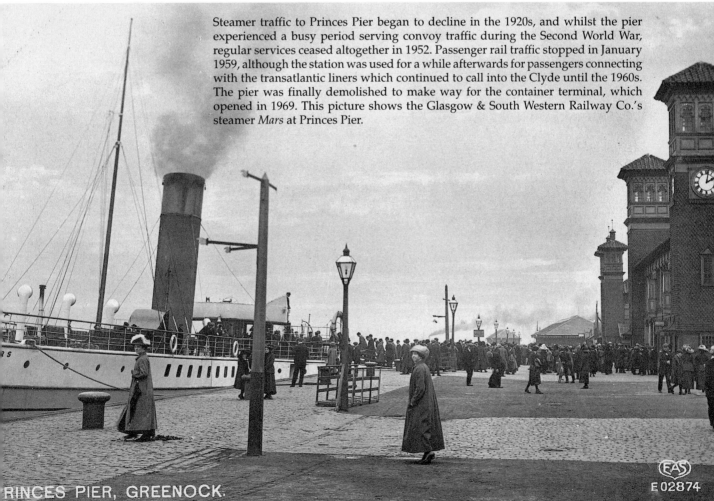

Steamer traffic to Princes Pier began to decline in the 1920s, and whilst the pier experienced a busy period serving convoy traffic during the Second World War, regular services ceased altogether in 1952. Passenger rail traffic stopped in January 1959, although the station was used for a while afterwards for passengers connecting with the transatlantic liners which continued to call into the Clyde until the 1960s. The pier was finally demolished to make way for the container terminal, which opened in 1969. This picture shows the Glasgow & South Western Railway Co.'s steamer *Mars* at Princes Pier.

RINCES PIER, GREENOCK.

E 02874

Sandringham Terrace   535.

The four-storey block of 1–12 Sandringham Terrace occupies the part of the Esplanade between Margaret Street and Fox Street and stretches back to include the low numbers in both these streets. The flats were built in the early 1900s on the site of the old mansion of Seafield, formerly the residence of local merchant Alexander R. Johnston. William Strachan of the Baltic Sawmills in Mearns Street was a timber merchant and builder who specialised in the construction of high quality tenements; this project was one of his many property developments in the west of Scotland. Those in Greenock included Queen Alexandra Mansions (p88), and properties at Bank Street, Trafalgar Street and South Street, plus the block of flats at the corner of Ardgowan Street and Patrick Street. Several of the Sandringham closes were notable for their decorative tiles manufactured by J. Dean Ltd. of Glasgow representing scenes of the Clyde hills, steamers and yachts.

One of the most far-sighted town planning projects in nineteenth century Greenock was the creation of the Esplanade. A plan for such a facility was first drawn up in 1857, but no action was taken until 1863, when Provost Grieve proposed that the soil from the then massive excavations of the Albert Harbour be used to create a continuation of Clyde Street from Campbell Street to Fort Matilda 'so as to form a fine Esplanade'. At that time the area was still rough shore ground and the few houses built on the proposed line of the esplanade sat literally on the head of the beach. Consent for the project was obtained from Sir Michael Shaw Stewart and the existing feuars, and work commenced in 1864 with estimated costs being £12,000. The Esplanade was completed in July 1867 at a final cost of £18,248. This figure caused some councillors to complain that the scheme had crippled the finances of the council, and the money might have been better spent on general improvements elsewhere in the town. However, others were of the opinion that the actual cost was nothing compared to the advantages that would result from the development. Henry 'Birdie' Bowers was born in 1883 in the large house at the corner of North Street at a time when there were still only a few isolated villas on the Esplanade. A member of Captain Robert Scott's ill-fated expedition to the South Pole, 'Birdie' Bowers died with Scott and his companions on the return trip from the pole towards the end of March 1912. This picture shows the western section of the Esplanade.

The Boat Clubhouse at the west end of the Esplanade with a G&SWR steamer – either *Mercury* or *Neptune* – on the river.

The inauguration of the West of Scotland Amateur Boat Club (later Royal West Boat Club) took place on Saturday 30 June 1866 at the recently erected clubhouse at Fort Matilda. According to newspaper reports at the time, the weather on the day was not very favourable – in fact it was so wet in the morning that it was considered advisable to postpone the opening ceremony. However, about four o'clock around a dozen of the club's boats were launched – including gigs, jolly boats and outrigger skiffs – and together with the club's barge proceeded upriver witnessed by a considerable number of spectators from the shore. The boats then turned to head back at HMS *Lion*, but due to deteriorating weather conditions the proposed line of a procession was abandoned and an informal race back to the clubhouse took place. The state of the weather also prevented the boats making a planned circuit through Gourock bay. The handsome brick clubhouse was built for about £200 and had accommodation for 25 boats. On its opening day the club had 15 boats and 94 members.

S/S "Dunara Castle" ashore Battery Point Greenock 29th Augt 1922

Between 4 and 5 a.m. on 29 August 1922 the West Highland steamer *Dunara Castle* ran ashore at the Battery Point, just west of the torpedo factory pier. The vessel, carrying a hundred passengers and a cargo of livestock, was proceeding upriver when, to avoid colliding with a tug, she changed course so severely that she ran aground. The weather at the time was perfectly calm, but as the tide receded the boat took a heavy list to port, causing concern for the safety of the passengers, the majority of whom were tourists returning from the West Highlands. However, they were quickly conveyed from the scene by motor boat to Princes Pier and Gourock Pier. After the passengers had been safely landed, the crew set to work to deal with the large number of sheep on board, and these were also safely transported to Gourock throughout the day. The *Dunara Castle*, built in 1875 by Blackwood & Gordon at Port Glasgow, appeared relatively undamaged, and not surprisingly was an object of considerable interest to sightseers at the Battery Park on the day of the incident.

In 1907 the Admiralty compulsorily purchased about ten acres of land and four and three quarter acres of foreshore at Battery Park from Sir Hugh Shaw Stewart as a site for the Clyde Torpedo Factory. This was designed to produce a special class of torpedo to meet the requirements of modern naval warfare, and after construction at Greenock the torpedoes were to be tested in Loch Long. 700 workers from the Royal Naval torpedo factory at Woolwich Arsenal were transferred to Greenock as part of the plan. The original buildings opened in 1910 and were made of freestone from the nearby Gourock quarries. The main single-storey structure covered about 6,000 square yards, with ancillary buildings including workshops, experimental cells and pickling tanks. During and after the First World War the Greenock works carried out both the design and manufacture of torpedoes, but at the outbreak of the Second

World War in 1939 design work was stopped and all effort put into making torpedoes for the war. At this stage between three and four thousand people were employed in the factory. Towards the end of the war development of new torpedoes was reintroduced, but shortly afterwards the decision was taken to transfer all production to Alexandria. Greenock remained as a centre for the research and design of torpedoes until the establishment closed in 1959. The original ground at the Battery Park had been accessible to the public for many years, and Sir Hugh Shaw Stewart donated a portion of its purchase price to the town council to help preserve the remainder of the area as an open space for community use. Some years later, in 1914, ownership of the park was transferred to the council. The upper picture shows the site chosen for the torpedo factory, seen from the Lyle Road, while the lower one shows the factory itself.

Eldon Street was originally known as the Low Gourock Road, and as the main route from Greenock to Gourock it became a turnpike road around 1804. Turnpikes were operated by road trustees, with tolls levied on carriages, carts and horse-drawn vehicles (mail coaches were exempt from payment). The income from the tolls was used for road maintenance, but the total operation remained in deficit with, for instance, figures for 1822 showing an annual income of £13,702, annual expenditure of £8,057, and debt standing at £109,962. Toll bars were let out annually by the trust, and in the Greenock area were situated at Brachelston, Crawfurdsdyke, Low Gourock and Common Craig. The toll house opposite the Battery Park (pictured) dates from the early nineteenth century. In 1838 460 tolls were collected on this stretch of road, the number rising to 1,220 in 1865 and 1,402 in 1872.

In August 1910 plans were unveiled for houses to be built by William H. Kirkwood at the foot of Lyle Road, immediately west of Fort Matilda station. The scheme consisted of a block of ten self-contained dwelling houses, eight of which were of five apartments, the two end ones having six apartments. The site was described as a very eligible one, offering an extensive view of the firth, and all houses would have a good garden area at the back. As the Dean of Guild had passed the plans, construction work would start immediately. Nearby Fort Matilda station was built as a stop on the Caledonian Railway's extension line from Greenock to Gourock. Construction work on the western section of the line was carried out by Hugh Kennedy & Son of Partick, and began in 1885. The line required a large iron bridge to be thrown across Lyle Road, which was re-routed straight down to Eldon Street. The one and a half mile railway tunnel extending from Drums Farm to Inverkip Street was started on 11 March 1888, and employed 30–40 men on each face with work continuing night and day. The excavations from the tunnel were used to form the railway embankment to Gourock bay.

Throughout the nineteenth century many large mansions were built in the west end of the town by various merchants, shipbuilders, sugar refiners and other entrepreneurs. One of the furthest west was Whitefarland on Octavia Terrace overlooking the site of the former battery at Fort Matilda. The house was built in grey granite in 1872 by Walter Robert Kinniple, the civil engineer who was appointed by the harbour trustees to design and oversee the construction of the James Watt Dock complex (p5). It was said that Mr Kinniple was a man of great ideas and professional ability, and that for twenty years he was the most prominent and influential person in the town. During the First World War Whitefarland was requisitioned by the military and used by the Argyll and Sutherland Highlanders. In 1920 it came on to the market and was purchased by Mr A. S. Kerr of the Glebe sugar refinery. By 1967 the house was becoming unmanageable, and the original Whitefarland was demolished, to be replaced by a modern building on the same site. The upper picture shows a carriage outside the original Whitefarland, while the lower one illustrates a corner of the ballroom, which was added to the house later by Mr Kinniple to provide entertainment for his three daughters.

One of the most notable buildings in the West End is the Sir Gabriel Wood Mariners' Asylum in Newark Street. Gourock-born Gabriel Wood had a successful career as a ship owner and civil servant in the diplomatic service, with postings to locations including the United States, West Indies and Canada, as a result of which he was knighted in 1825. Throughout his life he contributed regularly to several Greenock charities, but his most generous act was to bequeath the residue of his estate to provide an institution in Greenock for aged and destitute seamen. As a result the Mariners' Asylum was built on seven acres of ground at

Opposite: With a move westwards from the town centre favoured by ship owners, merchants and manufacturers in the nineteenth century, several large mansions and villas with extensive grounds and gardens were built on Newark Street, formerly the Gourock High Road. Balclutha became the home of Robert L. Scott of Scotts' shipbuilding company, and at one time the mansions of Dungourney, Bellaire and Stoneleigh were occupied by various members of the Caird shipbuilding family. In this photograph, Bellaire, the home of Patrick Caird, is on the right, while the larger house to the left was Stoneleigh, latterly the home of Arthur Caird. Stoneleigh was demolished in 1948 and became the site of

Newark Street at a cost of £8,383 10s., and opened on 17 October 1854. The intention of the home at the time was to allow the 'reception of 50 aged and decayed merchant master mariners and merchant seamen, natives of Renfrew, Ayr, Dunbarton, Argyll and Bute, who should have attained the age of 55 years and be of good character'. Further bequests were forthcoming from Sir Gabriel Wood's family, and in 1893 the sum of £778 18s. 11d. was received from the American government as compensation for the loss of ships which Gabriel Wood had owned when he lived in Maryland, and which had been captured during the war with the French.

several council houses. West of Stoneleigh was Lindores, which belonged to Alexander Lyle of the Lyle Shipping Company. Across the street from the mansions is Finnart St Paul's Church, built as St Paul's at the request of west end residents of the West Parish. The original church, erected in 1878 at the top of Bentinck Street, was an iron building, but this was replaced in 1893 by a larger stone structure costing £12,000. It was opened by John Caird, Principal of Glasgow University, a member of the local shipbuilding family who had chosen an academic career rather than join the family business. The congregation of St Paul's united with that of nearby Finnart Church in 1978.

In 1878, during an unprecedented downturn in trade, the Police Board agreed to a suggestion from Provost Abram Lyle that a road should be opened up over the Lyle Hill, thus providing work for many men and their families who had no means of financial support. The board also agreed later that the completed road should become known as Lyle Road. Work began on 3 December 1878 with thirty-one men employed from eight until four at the rate of 1s. 8d. per day. By the end of December the workforce had increased to 383, and throughout 1879 the average number of men employed was 280. In addition to this, forty stone breakers were employed. The length of the road from Madeira Street to Gourock Toll was one and three quarter miles, and it was laid off as a regular macadamised street to sixty feet in width. The final costs were about £12,500 in wages and £3,000 for plant and material. At the official opening of Lyle Road to the public on 1 May 1880, it was agreed that the new thoroughfare (foreground) offered unsurpassed views over the River Clyde, and hopes were expressed that part of it would be feued as a residential quarter of the town.

Opposite: Like many streets in the West End, Kelly Street was laid out in the latter part of the nineteenth century to provide reasonable housing away from the congested conditions of the town centre for Greenock's increasing population. It was named after the Kelly estate at Wemyss Bay, which was the home of Robert Wallace, Greenock's first MP following the Reform Act of 1832. He won the seat by a majority of 231 votes over local sugar refiner John Fairrie and held it for thirteen years, during which time he was a great supporter of the introduction of the penny post. Wallace had grand plans to expand his estate at Kelly to create a marine village with 200 villas plus churches, schools and extensive leisure facilities. However, his ambitious plans led to such extreme losses that he had to sell the estate. A later owner of Kelly estate was Dr James 'Paraffin' Young, whose experiments with the distillation of shale to yield paraffin established his reputation as an early oil technologist. Just outwith the picture at the top of Kelly Street was the Caddlehill Steam Laundry, which first opened *c.*1895. In 1943 the original building was destroyed by fire, but due to the importance of its work for HM Forces permission to rebuild it was granted and it reopened in December 1944.

South Street was originally called Ford Road because of the stepping stones (later bridge) which at one time were required to cross the West Burn as it flowed through the Brachelston Square area. There was also a farm steading named Ford located in the area between present day upper Kelly Street and Caddlehill Street. When proposals for a cemetery in this area were being discussed in 1845, it was suggested that the street be widened and improved so that the entrance to the cemetery could be created between the bridge and Brachelston quarry. It was some time later, from about the 1870s onwards, that tenemental properties began to appear on South Street, Nelson Street and in the surrounding areas, providing housing outwith the central area of the town for the increasing number of better paid artisans, semi-skilled and clerical workers.

In 1845 the town council asked for a report on the provision of a new burial ground for Greenock, as a result of which a site on the road to Inverkip was proposed. This was considered most suitable, as it was a secluded situation and out of view of the river. The site in question was seventeen acres of land bounded by Bow Farm on the west and Inverkip Road to the south, owned by Mr McFarlane of the Ford. As a result the Greenock Cemetery Company was formed in 1846 and proceeded to lay out the ground. Following early objections to the possible use of the word Necropolis in the title, the council resolved that for all time coming the name should simply be the Cemetery. The cast iron gates in Greek revival style (right) which were erected at the entrance in 1847 were designed by the architect Charles Wilson and cast at McCulloch & Co.'s iron foundry. Also prominent in this picture of Brachelston Square is Orangefield Baptist Church, which opened for worship in May 1878. The spacious new church had accommodation for 650 people and had been completed in less than a year at a cost of £5,000. The origins of the congregation date back to 1806 when meetings of Baptists were held with visiting ministers at the foot of West Quay Lane. The first settled minister was appointed in 1819, and over the years congregations met in various locations including Sir Michael Street, and latterly the Nelson Street chapel until Orangefield was built.

For many years Greenock's south-westerly development stopped at the cemetery gates at Brachelston Square. Beyond that the road to Inverkip followed the line of the West Burn as it flowed towards the town, with very few buildings other than farms. The names of many of these farms were used in the various housing schemes which developed later in the south-west area, including Bow, Pennyfern, Fancy Farm, Auchneagh, Larkfield and Flatterton. This photograph shows the edge of the cemetery and the bottom of Bow Road on the right as it joins Inverkip Road. On the brow of the hill in the distance are the buildings of Everton Farm.

In 1908 Sir Hugh Shaw Stewart gave six acres of ground on Inverkip Road to Greenock Corporation to create a recreation facility for local children, and at the same time provide relief work during a period of high unemployment. Work began in October, and at times employed up to 128 men on the site, averaging fifty employees on the second phase of the project. The Lady Alice Park was opened on 27 May 1910 by Lady Alice Shaw Stewart, after whom it was named. A varied programme of sports for children was organised, including team events for local schools. The original intention was that the first section opened would be set aside for children's recreation, and that provision would later be made for a six rink bowling green. In the event two bowling greens were laid out, and additional ground was granted for the

children's play area. Over fifty years later the ground to the east of the bowling greens was chosen as the site for new public swimming baths. The idea was first approved by the council in 1952, but difficulty in obtaining the necessary capital finance delayed a start on construction until 1963. It was agreed that the facility should be named after the late Hector McNeil, Greenock's MP from 1941 to 1955 and Secretary of State for Scotland 1950–51. The baths were finally completed in 1966 at a cost of £320,000, and opened on 19 February that year when Scottish Olympic swimmer Bobby McGregor was invited to swim the first two lengths in the pool. The Hector McNeil baths closed in 1996 when swimming facilities transferred to the new Waterfront Complex, and the building was subsequently demolished.

When this photograph was taken in 1979 these were the last prefabs remaining in Greenock, situated at the corner of Thom Street and Old Inverkip Road. At the end of the Second World War, one solution to replacing housing damaged during the Blitz was to use temporary houses, and the town was given an allocation of 800 prefabricated homes. Many of these prefabs, constructed from steel and aluminium, came from America, while others were built from war-damaged aircraft. They provided well-designed accommodation with mod cons of fitted kitchens, hot running water, electric appliances and an inside bathroom. The first prefabs were erected and occupied at Bridgend, and other sites were prepared at Peat Road, Bow Farm, Auchneagh and Inverkip Road opposite Ravenscraig Hospital. Prefabs turned out to be more durable and popular that anyone had foreseen, and were an important factor in establishing post war standards in 'modern' living. This site is now occupied by a number of modern houses.

In 1921 the council identified the Inverkip Valley as a suitable place to build 1,200 new houses to alleviate overcrowding in the town centre. Following the Housing Act of 1924 it agreed to use sites at Bow Farm, Hole Farm and Cowdenknowes, as well as Bridgend, to take advantage of government subsidies of £9 per house for forty years to replace slum dwellings. 204 houses were erected at Bow Farm and a further 148 at High Bow under the Slum Areas 1930 and 1935 schemes. The need for a branch library to serve the growing south-west area was acknowledged in 1930, and on 10 February 1933 the South West Library opened with a stock 12,000 books and a large newsroom facility. Two months later, across Inverkip Road, Lady Alice Primary School (illustrated here) was opened by Lady Alice Shaw Stewart. At the time it was described as one of the best-equipped and most attractively laid out schools in Scotland.

Additional hospital accommodation separate from Greenock Infirmary was first proposed by the medical officer in 1899. When Greenock and District Combination Hospital opened at Gateside on 3 January 1908 it was situated well out in the country, precisely because it was built as an isolation hospital for the most common infectious diseases of the time – enteric fever, typhus, diphtheria, measles and scarlet fever. Initially it had 120 beds, with separate pavilions for different diseases and a further forty-four beds proposed for scarlet fever. There was also provision for the observation of doubtful cases, and separate isolation in cases of double infection. The site at Gateside covered six acres and was acquired for £5,500, with the project costing £70,000. Gateside closed in 1979 when it was incorporated into the new Inverclyde Royal Hospital, and the former site is now used for housing.

In the 1920s proposals for an auxiliary hospital were discussed with a view to relieving the strain on the Royal Infirmary by providing convalescent facilities. The project became feasible as a result of a donation of £20,000 from Miss Rankin and Mr Matthew Rankin of the engineering firm Rankin & Blackmore. Following this, a further £40,000 was raised by community fund-raising by 1926. A site in the countryside was obtained to the west of the second Larkfield Road, described as being 'amid the pure and health-giving air of the Kip Valley', and in early 1930 Larkfield Hospital admitted its first patients. The hospital had two wards, each with ten beds, and also provided eighteen private rooms for those willing to pay moderate fees. Whilst originally intended mainly for convalescence, Larkfield had begun to take all medical cases by 1943, leaving the Royal Infirmary in the town centre as a surgical hospital. In July 1979 local hospital facilities were centralised on the adjacent site at Inverclyde Royal Hospital and Larkfield Hospital was closed.

In August 1950 a corporation housing report revealed that 6,000 new houses were required in Greenock to alleviate all cases of overcrowding and unfit accommodation, including provision for subtenants and families living in requisitioned dwellings. At the same time the council passed plans for a scheme of nearly 300 houses to be built in Larkfield, with another 400 projected for the area. In November 1952 the thousandth permanent house to have been built since the end of the Second World War was completed at Cumberland Road

and opened to the public as a show house. A valuable contribution to the rehousing programme was also being made by the Scottish Special Housing Association which had built 564 houses in Greenock at sites including Pennyfern and Larkfield. In 1957 further developments were approved for Branchton and Larkfield, and by 1960 Greenock Corporation had built 5,000 houses throughout the town since 1946. This view over Cumberland Road was taken in 1971 to show the start of construction work for Inverclyde Royal Hospital.

Following the introduction of the 1845 Poor Law, Greenock's first permanent poorhouse was built in Captain Street by the recently appointed parochial board. 'Lunatic wards' were added later. By the 1870s the building was in such disrepair that the parochial board decided to build a new poorhouse (illustrated here) at Smithston, at that time a considerable distance from the town. Smithston Poorhouse and Asylum opened in March 1879 with accommodation for 500 paupers and 200 lunatics under the supervision of a governor and a resident doctor. The £122,900 cost of the project outraged many ratepayers who referred to the new institution as 'the palace of the Kip Valley'. Fear of the poorhouse remained a factor in many people's lives well into the twentieth century, even after the introduction of national systems of benefits such as non-contributory old age pensions (1908)

and National Insurance (1911). In 1920–21, for example, there were still 182 people in the poorhouse together with 186 patients in the asylum. Smithston was designated as a poorhouse and asylum until 1940, but over a period of time many improvements were made to the buildings and in the professional care of patients. The complex was requisitioned in 1939 and used by the Canadian Navy as HMCS Niobe. In 1947 it was restored to its original use, and at the introduction of the National Health Service was renamed Ravenscraig Hospital.

A major part of the Kip Valley housing scheme included the developments at Cowdenknowes and Cornhaddock. The ideal types of houses suggested were self-contained cottages, but due to a shortage of land the corporation agreed to the inclusion of three-storey tenements in some areas as a reasonable and economical solution to the housing problem. There was also approval for the four in a block style of house first exhibited in Edinburgh in 1886, comprising two-storey blocks with two houses on each floor. All would include adequate-sized rooms and passageways, hot and cold running water, baths, and probably electricity. Under the 1919 (Assisted) Scheme, Greenock built 150 houses at Cowdenknowes, 52 at Cornhaddock and 120 at Cornhaddock Upper. By April 1923 the latest batch of houses at Cornhaddock were of the tenement type, with the block on the railway side almost ready for tenants. The Cowdenknowes area had been transformed by August 1925 with the formation of several new streets and an important new thoroughfare to be called Dunlop Street, laid out on land which until recently had been pasture for cattle. In 1928 the education authority bought ground at Dunlop Street for a new secondary school, and Greenock High School opened on 12 June 1931 having cost an estimated £80,000. Twenty classrooms provided accommodation for 710 pupils, plus spacious rooms for geography, sewing, science and metalwork. The extensive site also allowed provision of playgrounds, a hockey pitch and a football pitch. The upper picture shows a general view of the Kip Valley Housing Scheme, while the lower one features the top of Dunlop Street from Cornhaddock Street.

Taken just below the Wemyss Bay railway line, this view looks down from Peat Road over Dunlop Street. Six houses within the Cornhaddock and Cowdenknowes council housing schemes at the corner of Dunlop Street and Murdieston Street were built under the auspices of the Scottish Veterans Garden City Association. The association had offered to inaugurate a programme of housing for disabled ex-servicemen in Greenock, undertaking to build the houses and defray the capital costs, after which they would be available for rent at four shillings per week for a four-room house. Greenock Corporation suggested a site at Cornhaddock where six houses could be erected and the first foundation stone was laid in June 1921. The later site of the ambulance depot, built in 1965 to replace accommodation in a hut beside the Royal Infirmary, was behind the houses. The new garage was built on several allotments and had space for twelve ambulances, plus offices and servicing facilities. When the ambulance service moved to its new depot at Knowe Road in 2000, the premises were taken over by a veterinary practice.

This view from above Peat Road shows the original site of St Columba's RC Secondary School, formally opened on 15 June 1933 by His Grace the Archbishop of Glasgow, the Revd Donald Mackintosh. The building had been completed at a cost of £50,000, a sum which included all furniture and fittings and the making of adjacent roads. It was built within a year, and considered to be one of the best-equipped schools in the country. In June 1971 the 1,320 pupils of St Columba's High School moved to a new campus at Bayhill in Gourock – the first school in Renfrewshire designed as an all-through comprehensive school and built at a cost of £1.25 million. For a number of years after this, the Peat Road building provided accommodation for Notre Dame High School until its move to the former Cowdenknowes building in Dunlop Street. The area is now the site of a large housing development.

Greenock's water supply originally came from streams including the West Burn, Delling Burn and Carts Burn, and from wells for domestic use sunk at locations throughout the town. In 1773 a limited piped water supply was installed to designs prepared by James Watt, but as the town expanded demand grew for improved water supplies, particularly for industrial premises. Robert Thom, a civil engineer from Rothesay, designed a scheme of carrying supplies from the Shaws Water above the town to Greenock via a nine kilometre aqueduct known as the Cut. On 10 June 1825 Shaws Water Joint Stock Company was incorporated with capital of £30,000, and on 16 April 1827 this major engineering project was officially opened. The enterprise was a huge success, with four industries – a grain mill, paper mill, power loom manufactory and sugar refinery – using the supply on the opening day. The scheme gave the town 21,000 cubic feet of water per day, and a further expansion of capacity was added in 1845 with the construction of the Kelly aqueduct. However, the primary object of the Shaws Water Company was to supply motive power to mills and industrial premises on the line of falls, and it was often unable to meet the needs of domestic users. The problem of domestic supply was not fully addressed until the completion of the Gryfe reservoir schemes in 1872.

Built to take full advantage of the new power supply provided by the Shaws Water Company, Overton paper mill opened on the same day as the Cut in April 1827, occupying falls Nos. 18 & 19. The mill (which also operated a warehouse close to the river at 4 Custom House Place) was built by James Walkinshaw, but in 1850 ownership passed to James Gray & Co., with William Brown and a Mr Dowdes as partners. When Mr Gray retired in 1856, the firm became Brown, Stewart & Co., and in 1892 was incorporated with Dalmarnock Mills in Glasgow. Overton paper mill was destroyed by fire in 1887, after which it was rebuilt and continued to operate until about 1930.

The great wheel in the Shaws water system was constructed *c.*1839 by James Smith of Deanston, Perthshire. In its day it was the largest waterwheel in the world, and was described as one of the most perfect specimens of its class. It weighed 180 tons and was 70 feet in diameter and 12 feet wide. The total height of the waterfalls was 69 feet, 4 inches, and the machinery developed 230 horsepower. The wheel made one and a third turns per minute and was used to power a cotton mill.

One famous company which took advantage of the Shaws water supply, utilising five falls, was the Merino Mills, built in 1840 at Drumfrochar by John Fleming and his brother-in-law James Reid. The mill was originally intended to produce worsted weaving yarns for Glasgow and Bradford manufacturers, but became known for the spinning of carpet yarns, knitting wool and hosiery. The first mill was destroyed by fire on 5 October 1880, throwing 500 people out of work. By then it had introduced a greatly admired system of half-time work for its female child workers as young as ten years of age, whereby girls worked and went to school on alternate days. A large new six-storey mill was rebuilt on the site within two years. This was 220 feet long and 60 feet in breadth, with knitting sheds, warehouses and washhouses also on the site. The addition of three more falls by the water company increased the power supply. At its peak Fleming & Reid's employed 1,500 workers at the mill, 1,300 of whom were women. From a single retail outlet in Greenock, it also developed a chain of over 200 knitting wool shops throughout Britain. Latterly it became part of Paton & Baldwin, but following reductions in the workforce finally closed in 1981. The upper picture shows the view over Murdieston dam and the cemetery with the original Merino Mills in the foreground. The lower picture is of the rebuilt Merino Mills of 1882.

In 1834 an informal survey of the Highland population in Greenock revealed that between 300 and 500 children of Highland parents did not attend school. As a result the Highlanders' Church and School Association resolved to undertake the building and endowment of a school for the children of Highlanders in Greenock and vicinity. Fund-raising began, and a site was acquired in Roxburgh Street for an infant and juvenile school. Both schools opened in July 1835, with fees ranging from 1s. 6d. per quarter for infants to 4s. per quarter for reading, writing and arithmetic in the juvenile school. Each child was also charged 6d. coal money in two quarters of the year. In 1842 an additional storey was added for a commercial department, and an evening class for instruction in Gaelic was started. A large Sabbath school also operated. Around 1878 responsibility for the running of the Highlanders' Academy transferred to the recently formed school board. When the Caledonian Railway's line from Greenock to Gourock was approved in the 1880s the proposed route via the West station involved the demolition of the original Highlanders' Academy building (above). A site for a replacement school (below) was acquired at Mount Pleasant Street, and in December 1887 the new Highlanders' Academy opened at a cost of £15,000, which was met by compensation from the railway company. The opening day of the new school was not without controversy. The school board had declined to reappoint the existing head teacher Robert Wilson to the new school, and instead gave the job to William Cook from Mearns Street School. On the morning of 4 December 1887, several hundred children assembled under the supervision of Mr Wilson at the old poorhouse in Captain Street, and at nine o'clock set off behind three pipers to march to the new school via Holmscroft Street. At the same time a public demonstration in support of Mr Wilson gathered momentum, and it was estimated that between 8,000 and 9,000 people lined the route of the march. When Robert Wilson reached the new school he was refused entry, leading to discontent in the crowd which stormed the building. Chaos reigned for about an hour until the situation was brought under control by the police, who made several arrests. A number of parents were later charged with assault.

Queen Alexandra Mansions and West Station, Greenock

For many years the Caledonian Railway sought to extend its line from its terminus at Cathcart Street, Greenock, to Gourock, allowing a better link-up with steamer services to the Clyde coast towns. Eventually a route was agreed and construction began in the 1880s, with the West station being built at the corner of Inverkip Street and Newton Street. The plans were described as showing a 'very neat and substantial stone building in Renaissance style', and provided a booking hall with two entrances from Inverkip Street, a stationmaster's room, one general waiting room and two first class waiting rooms for ladies and gentlemen respectively. The line opened in June 1889. Situated across Newton Street from the station, Queen Alexandra Mansions were completed c.1906 by the property developer William Strachan. The block was a mixture of flats and commercial properties, including MacSymon's general grocer's store, Mitchell & Hall (drapers), J. G. Taylor photographic suppliers, a plumber, baker, and the Alexandra tea rooms. In 1912 Greenock Provident Bank opened its South West (later West Station) branch at 1 Newton Street, moving into the corner property in 1924. In due course the bank occupied the entire site from the corner of Newton Street to 46 Inverkip Street.

In 1806 the need for an isolation hospital for the town was expressed by Dr Speirs, surgeon at the Dispensary for the Sick Poor at Cathcart Street. It was felt that the facility would be required in the event of an outbreak of typhus fever, but as the project developed it was decided to extend the proposal to become a general hospital or infirmary. A site near the burial ground at Inverkip Street was acquired, and the establishment admitted its first patient on 2 May 1809. Over the years extensions were added, but by 1866 the population of Greenock had increased so greatly that it was agreed a new facility was required. This opened in March 1868, at a time when nurses trained in the Nightingale system first appeared (by 1871 21 such nurses were employed). The building seen here – with various alterations and adaptations – continued to serve the community for another hundred years. Greenock Royal Infirmary closed in July 1979 when facilities transferred to the new Inverclyde Royal Hospital. The building was demolished in May 1983, and the site developed for a sheltered housing complex.

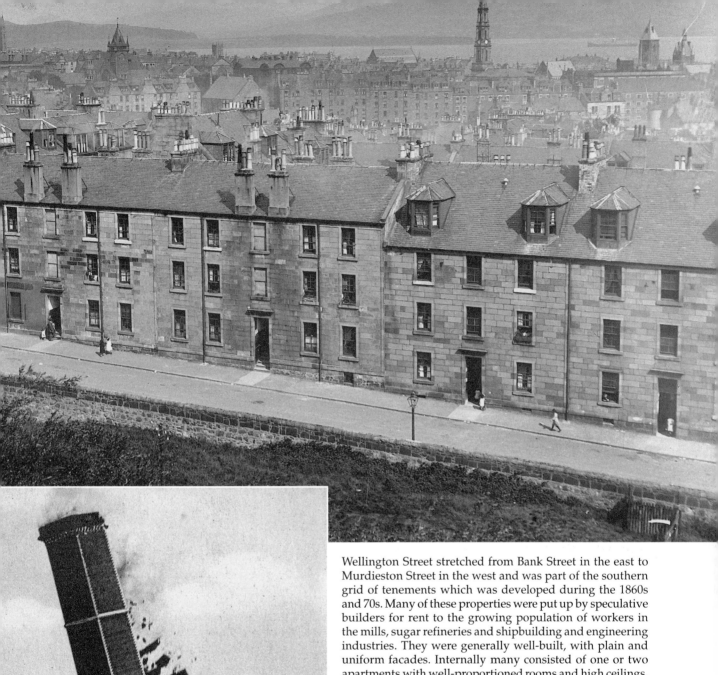

Wellington Street stretched from Bank Street in the east to Murdieston Street in the west and was part of the southern grid of tenements which was developed during the 1860s and 70s. Many of these properties were put up by speculative builders for rent to the growing population of workers in the mills, sugar refineries and shipbuilding and engineering industries. They were generally well-built, with plain and uniform facades. Internally many consisted of one or two apartments with well-proportioned rooms and high ceilings, and at the time were a vast improvement on conditions in the town centre. However, in later years, many of the houses fell below reasonable standards for reasons such as overcrowding, shared toilet facilities, and general structural deterioration. As a result much of the area was demolished and rebuilt from the late 1960s onwards. Greenock Health Centre in nearby Holmscroft Street was opened in 1982.

The first Roxburgh Street sugar refinery was built in 1832 and operated until 1865 when its then owners, James Richardson & Co., pulled it down and re-erected a new building on the site. This remained in use until 1896 when the firm was wound up and the refinery sold and demolished. The 160-foot high chimney, however, remained a local landmark for some years. According to the *Greenock Telegraph*, thousands of spectators watched its demolition on 8 April 1909. At about 11.15 a.m. explosives were fired, instantly felling the stack into the old refinery grounds towards Duncan Street. Besides the crowds which gathered in the neighbourhood, spectators lined the slopes of Prospecthill for a fine view of the demolition. **89**

A popular thoroughfare leading down to the town centre, Ann Street was reputedly named after Ann Bearhope who originally leased ground in the area for a market garden. As the street developed it became a busy mix of tenemental property combined with shops and small businesses. On the right is the former South Kirk, which disjoined from the West Parish in 1875 to serve the growing population in the area. Built at a cost of £5,000, it remained in use until 1965 when it united with the Mount Park Church in Trafalgar Street to

The 1872 Education (Scotland) Act dealt almost exclusively with elementary education, and did not address the question of free secondary schooling. For many years some advanced teaching was offered in small departments in elementary schools, but there was no separate provision for higher grade education in the town, except at Greenock Academy which was fee-paying. In September 1903 Greenock School Board opened a higher grade school (illustrated here) on a site adjoining Holmscroft School, bounded by Trafalgar, Wellington and Dempster Streets. It cost £21,223 and provided accommodation for 980 pupils in seventeen classrooms, plus two central halls and a gymnasium. On the

become South Park. The building was bought by the education authority as an extension to the Mount School and was subsequently demolished for the construction of Grovepark (later) Wellington High School. Just behind the church was Holmscroft School, which opened on 5 March 1888 without formal ceremony when up to 600 pupils moved from the old Sir Michael Street School, another building that was demolished to make way for the railway extension to Gourock. Holmscroft was demolished in 1968.

upper floor there were science labs and rooms for technical education, plus a large cookery room. In 1931 a new High School building was opened at Dunlop Street, and the Dempster Street building was renamed the Mount School, becoming a junior secondary school for boys. Following an announcement in 1970, the Mount School closed and its pupils were transferred to the High School in Dunlop Street, which in turn became Cowdenknowes High School. The old school was demolished, and a new secondary school called Grovepark opened on the combined Holmscroft / Mount School site in June 1977. This later merged with Cowdenknowes to become Wellington Academy.

In 1855 a group of gentlemen from Wellington Park put forward a proposal for a new bowling green, and at a subsequent meeting on 5 October in Borland's Temperance Hotel the Grosvenor Bowling Club was founded. Among the founding members were Dugald McCall, grocer, Cathcart Street; Kenneth Cameron, grocer, 7 William Street; William Gaff, joiner of Mount Park Cottage; and James Innes Lang, merchant and ship owner of Brougham Street. Within a short period of time, a site at the top of Bank Street had been obtained from Sir Michael Shaw Stewart, and work on laying it out commenced. On 17 July 1856 the green was officially opened shortly after one o'clock, and despite showery conditions seventy-two players from various visiting clubs played an informal match in nine rinks. The total cost of the project, including the provision of a neat clubhouse, was between £500 and £600, and by the opening day the club had 130 members. It was named in honour of Lady Octavia Shaw Stewart, whose family name was Grosvenor.

In May 1852 members of the town council met with a deputation of local working men in the field at the head of Baker Street, which had been offered to the community as a playground by Sir Michael Shaw Stewart. It was agreed that the site had great potential to be laid out for different games, such as cricket, bowls and quoits. Shortly afterwards Wellington Park was opened with provision for a bowling green, cricket and football pitches, plus flower plots and pleasure grounds. In 1864 the construction of the Wemyss Bay railway line cut off a portion of the park to the south, which Sir Michael replaced with additional ground to the west. Unfortunately, in 1869, a section of the Glasgow & South Western Railway's line to Princes Pier also cut through the park, and once again Sir Michael made a further gift of land, thus maintaining facilities for a variety of sports at Wellington Park.

Proposals for a railway line to Wemyss Bay were developed to provide convenient access from Glasgow to several watering places on the coast. A scheme was put forward for a Greenock & Wemyss Bay Railway section of the Caledonian Railway, creating a line ten and a half miles in length branching off from the Caledonian's Greenock line half a mile west of Port Glasgow. Work commenced in November 1862, and the line opened to traffic on 15 May 1865 having cost £155,000. The first station on the line was Upper Greenock (illustrated here), situated near Berryyards Farm at the top of Lynedoch Street behind Anderson, Orr & Co.'s sugar refinery. The station was situated south of the line and approached from the street under a bridge via a neat carriage drive. After Upper Greenock the line continued to Inverkip and Wemyss Bay with halts at Ravenscraig and Dunrod. Upper Greenock station closed in 1967.

A serious accident occurred at Upper Greenock station at 4 p.m. on Thursday 11 July 1907. After leaving the siding at the station, the train attempted to stop at the level crossing at the Old Largs Road, but the brakes failed and it began to slip down the hill. The brakesman leapt off, but the driver and fireman remained on the footplate while the train gathered momentum, sweeping to the foot of the hill at a terrific pace. It crashed into the buffers with tremendous force, causing the locomotive to leap high in the air and fall on its side twenty feet beyond them, having ploughed its way over an embankment, jumped a small burn, and landed on the other side of the road which led to Wellington Bowling Club. Several men who were playing bowls at the time ran over to assist at the accident scene. Just prior to the collision with the buffers the driver and fireman finally jumped from the engine, but Mr Steel (the driver, of 13 Lauriston Street) suffered such severe injuries that he died shortly after being admitted to the Royal Infirmary. Mr McEwan, the fireman, was seriously injured but survived.

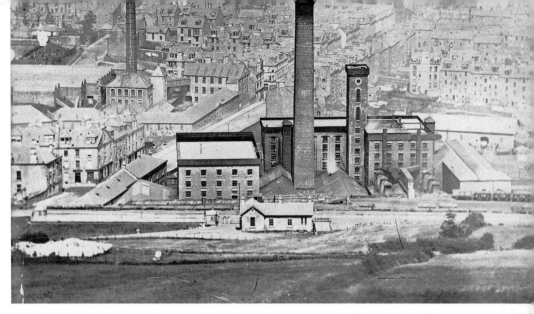

The view from behind the Wemyss Bay railway line at Upper Greenock looks down over the grid of tenements centred on Lynedoch Street and built from the 1870s onward. Westburn sugar refinery, at the top of Lynedoch Street, was first built as the Berryyards refinery in 1852 by Anderson, Orr & Co., and was operated by them until 1864. Some years later it was bought by Alex Scott & Sons who worked it until 1896. In that year Robert Kerr and his associates in the Brewers' Sugar Co. formed Westburn Sugar Refineries Ltd. and acquired Berryyards. Kerr's company operated a large refinery in Sugarhouse Lane on the site of the earliest large sugarhouse to have been built in Greenock (in 1765). His family also operated the Glebe refinery in Ker Street in the centre of the town. The Westburn refinery was seriously damaged in the Blitz on 7 May 1941, and remained out of action from then until November 1945. It traded as an independent company until 1964 when it became part of the Manbre & Garton group, which was taken over by Tate & Lyle in 1975. The last sugar refinery in Greenock, it closed in August 1997.

As a major ancillary industry to shipping and shipbuilding, several ropeworks developed in the Greenock area. The Greenock Ropework Co., for example, was established by Alexander Tough in East Regent Street in 1796, later operating from premises in Drumfrochar Road for many years. In 1898 the Birkmyre family of the Gourock Ropework Co. bought an old mill in Lynedoch Street, intending to operate it as a factory for producing binder twine. However, the outbreak of the Boer War meant that the War Office required large quantities of canvas goods such as marquees and bell tents, and the Lynedoch Street premises were turned over to war work as a matter of urgency. Young women employed in the piecework stitching of tents could earn more than thirty shillings per week, a fabulous wage in those days. After the Boer War, Lynedoch Street became the centre of the ropework's net-making activities, and power looms were introduced producing netting up to 35 feet in breadth and 100 to 200 yards in length. The products of the net-works went all over the world for a wide variety of uses, including fishing, agriculture, fruit growing, sport and transport. The Lynedoch Street factory finally closed in 1964, with the looms going to New Lanark and net work transferring to the Gourock Ropeworks in Port Glasgow.

The origins of Wellpark West Church date from December 1875 when a meeting was held to discuss the disjunction of a new congregation from the West Parish. By August 1876 it was reported in the *Greenock Advertiser* that the newly established church at the head of Bank Street was visible above its surroundings, and it was expected that the roof would be on before winter. Bazaars would take place throughout the year in the town hall to raise funds to complete the building. Twenty years earlier the site of the church had been occupied by nursery gardens. Wellpark

Church opened on 30 December 1877 with a sermon preached by Revd Dr McCulloch of the West Church. Shortly afterwards it was reported that there were 280 children in the Sunday school. The church was renamed Wellpark West in 1929 to distinguish it from the former Wellpark UF church at the foot of Lynedoch Street. It continued in use until 3 March 1996 when a final morning service was held, followed by a service of union in the Mid Kirk in the evening when the two congregations became Wellpark Mid Kirk. The site of Wellpark West Church is now occupied by a block of flats.

The Schaw family became associated with the lands of Greenock in the fourteenth century through marriage with the Galbraith family. When John Schaw obtained a royal charter in 1635 confirming Greenock as a burgh of barony his residence was described as 'new buildit'. It was known as the Mansion House, and stood above the town 'on an eminence, surrounded by pleasant parks and enclosures'. Originally no other feus were allowed within 300 yards of it. At one time the terraces on the brae leading down from the house towards Cross Shore Street held at least nine great guns. The house was altered and extended several times, the last extension taking place in 1740 when work was carried out by James Watt's

father. The Schaw family ceased to live in the Mansion House in 1756, although the business of the Greenock estate continued to be run from there for many years. It was demolished in 1886 as a result of construction work on the tunnel for the Caledonian Railway's line to Gourock, and was replaced by estate offices in the new Mansion House in

Union Street (p62). The Schaw family became connected to the Stewart family by marriage in the mid-eighteenth century, leading in time to the title Shaw Stewart of Greenock and Blackhall. The family home is now Ardgowan House at Inverkip, built between 1798 and 1801 to designs by the architect Hugh Cairncross.

In 1851 Sir Michael Shaw Stewart gifted five acres of ground beside the old Mansion House to the town. This was known as Well Park, and extended from Bank Brae on the west to St John's Brae on the east. The terms of the gift included preservation of the existing trees and the old well, after which the park was named. This was dated 1629 and was reckoned to be the oldest existing monument in Greenock. It had been built to provide a water supply for the Mansion House, and may also have commemorated the marriage of John Schaw to Helen Houston, as both their initials appear carved on the stonework. In 1852 plans for improving the layout and planting of the park were prepared by Stewart Murray of the Botanic Gardens in Glasgow, and were approved by the town council and Sir Michael. At that point he also agreed to include the terraces in his gift and a direct access route from Regent Street to Cathcart Street. After the First World War the park was chosen as the location for Greenock's war memorial. Following its completion, several improvements were made in 1926 including the installation of an imposing new entrance from Regent Street and a pathway to the memorial.

Regent Street stretches down to Delling Burn, the early informal boundary on the east of Greenock. It was part of one of the four approaches to the Mansion House, whose policies stretched from Ann Street in the west to the Carts Burn, and back towards Berryyards Farm to the south. Prominent in the picture is the spire of Wellpark Church, whose congregation dated back to 1737 when as a group of dissenters they worshipped in the open air. Their first church was built in Cartsdyke in 1745, and was replaced on the same location between Rue End and Stanners Streets in 1828, the building later becoming the first St Laurence's RC Church. Following the Disruption of 1843, the Wellpark congregation left the Established Church to form a Free Church,  building the new church at Wellpark in 1854. In 1900 this became a United Free Church before returning to the Church of Scotland in 1929. Fifty years later, in the face of a declining congregation, the church was forced to close, and the final service was held on 21 May 1979. The building lay unoccupied for several years, and following a serious fire only the steeple remained. This was demolished in 2002 when a block of flats was built on the site.

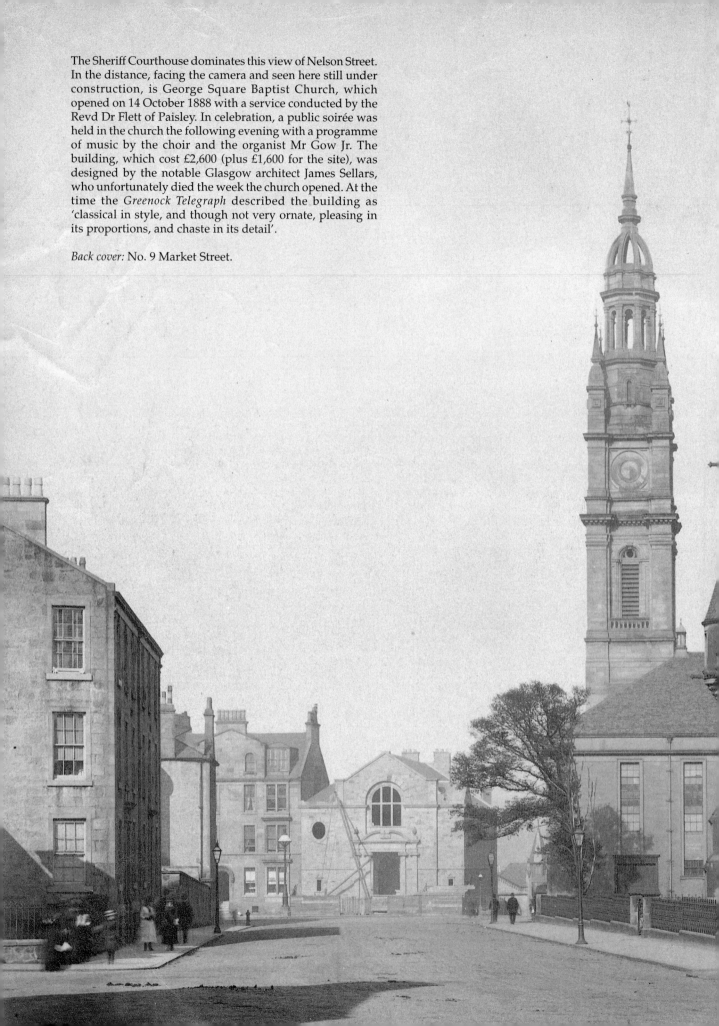

The Sheriff Courthouse dominates this view of Nelson Street. In the distance, facing the camera and seen here still under construction, is George Square Baptist Church, which opened on 14 October 1888 with a service conducted by the Revd Dr Flett of Paisley. In celebration, a public soirée was held in the church the following evening with a programme of music by the choir and the organist Mr Gow Jr. The building, which cost £2,600 (plus £1,600 for the site), was designed by the notable Glasgow architect James Sellars, who unfortunately died the week the church opened. At the time the *Greenock Telegraph* described the building as 'classical in style, and though not very ornate, pleasing in its proportions, and chaste in its detail'.

Back cover: No. 9 Market Street.